FRANK BOWLING

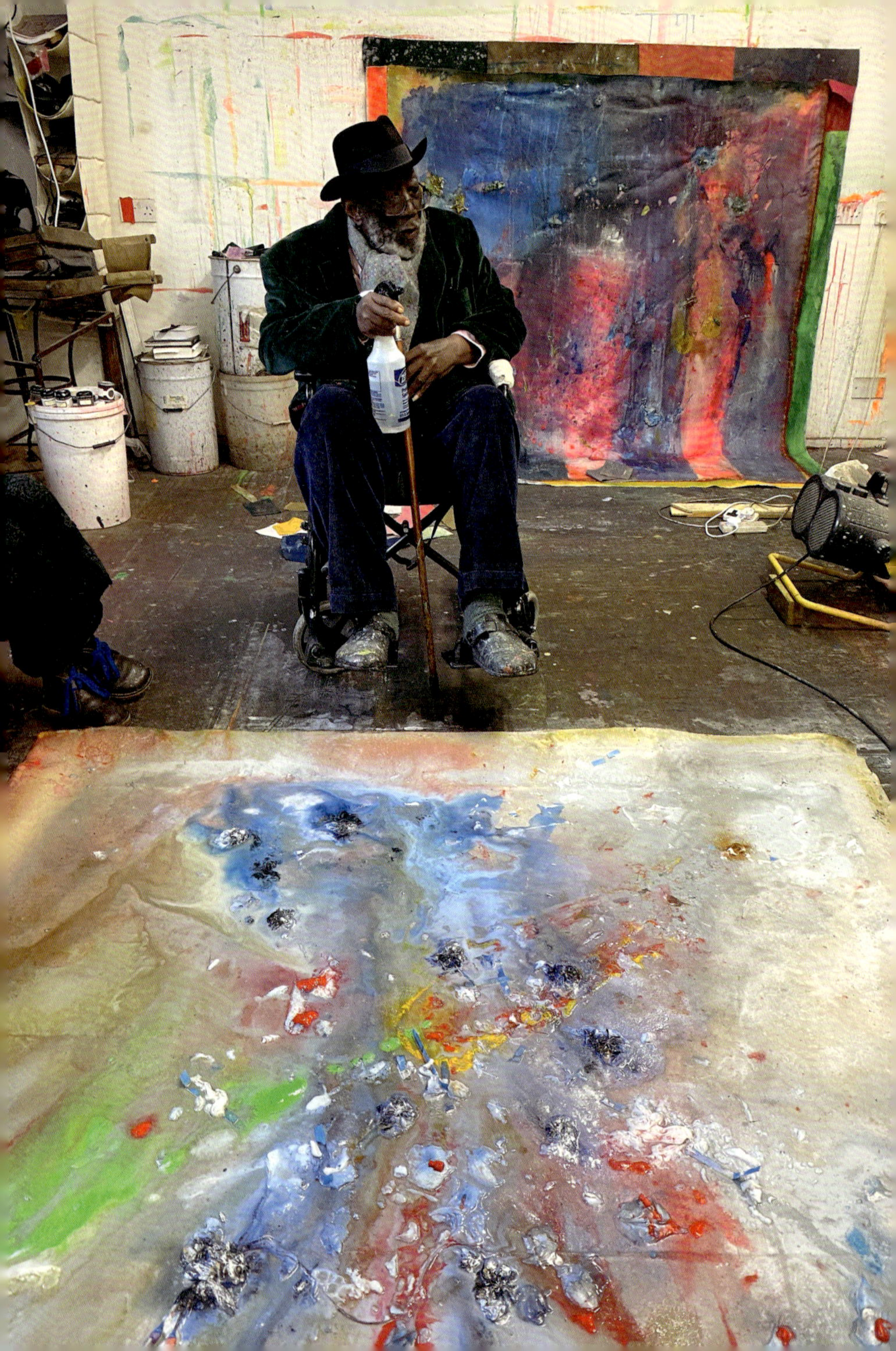

FRANK BOWLING

DOMINIQUE HEYSE-MOORE

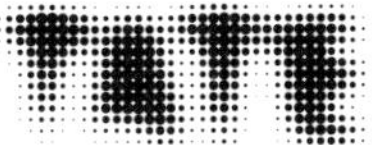

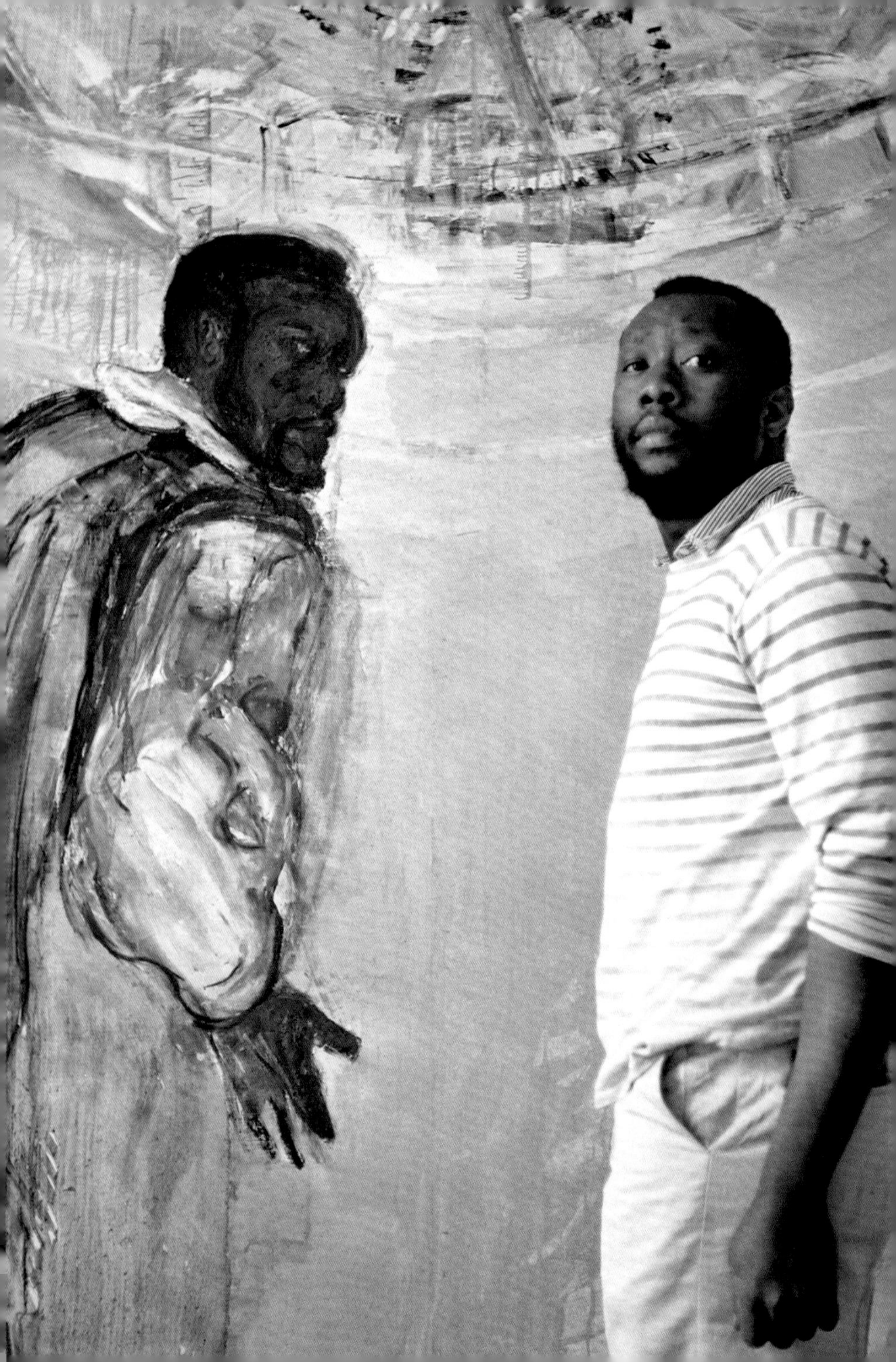

*The cotton duck canvas is tacked to its full length
and draped on the wall.
The polyether type foam is cut into strips and glued
to the canvas.
A ground colour is flooded into the canvas.*[1]

Two moments that took place in small pockets of London capture the sublime worlds created by Frank Bowling. The first involves a letter written by Rachel Scott to Tate Gallery in 1989 after the first acquisition of a work by Bowling, *Spreadout Ron Kitaj* 1984–6, into a national collection.[2] Some of these words begin this book, plainly describing the making of a painting in Bowling's studio, but when you look at any painting by the artist, so monumental they can envelope you, the anticipation built by Scott's account is palpable. This colourful flood, the new beginning of each canvas, establishes that Bowling's paintings have climate, they have catastrophic weather, they have atmosphere. This works at many scales, from the intimacy of the temperature of a studio, to the sultry light of a country, to the disobedience water displays to borders humans have drawn. These scales have been in the most spectacular tension across Bowling's long-standing art career: painting is personal, painting is about painting, painting is about the great shifts of history and culture. The drama is closely relatable and universally vast all at once.

The second moment came in 2019 when the art world gathered in Pimlico (the area in which Bowling lived during the 1960s and returned to in the 1980s) to celebrate the opening of the first major survey of Bowling's art at Tate Britain. Finally, six decades of breathtaking canvases were brought together in a journey through colour and its boundless climates. The mood was electric: it was one thrilling moment in the global shift of cultural weather patterns. The paintings themselves – *Raining Down South* 1968 (p.42) and *Towards Crab Island* 1983 (pp.80–1), to name a couple – are testament to Bowling's audacious ingenuity in negotiating a practice across cultures, conjuring all the earth, air and water that connects them.

All this happens through an enduring commitment to experiments with the colours, textures and flow of paint. The radical innovations of modern art in the twentieth century were formative for Bowling, particularly abstraction and expressionism. His work is usually described as abstract

Photograph of Frank Bowling with his 1962 *Self Portrait as Othello*, c.1965

because it is not necessarily a picture of something; in fact,
it is about the possibilities of paint. It is also often related
to expressionism because of the use of colours, forms and
gestures from which emotional experiences emerge. The
inclusion of recognisable subjects – such as maps, faces and
figures, buildings and landscapes, most often very intimate
to Bowling's own life and memories – has been central to the
development of a visual language deeply immersed in the wider
cultural debates of our times. Though he is best known for
large-scale paintings, his sculpture, writing, collage, teaching
and curating are also testament to a boundless creativity.

The art historian Kobena Mercer has described Bowling's
movements as an 'Atlantic Errantry',[3] evocative of a watery
and adventurous straying from a prescribed route. Born in
South America, Bowling studied and established himself as
an artist in England, and then in the US. The sociologist
Paul Gilroy made the influential rallying observation that there
is a culture – the Black Atlantic – that is African, American,
Caribbean and British all at once.[4] Bowling painted through
the midst of extraordinary decades of decolonisation and
reinvention in art, synthesising the two. He consistently
contained and overflowed the signifiers of decolonisation
with the vivid energy and liquid movement of paint. It is
unsurprising that maps have been such a recurrent form in
Bowling's work; they are an abstraction of a sense of place,
an opportunity for colour, and a testament to the seismic
changes of the twentieth century.

BOWLING'S VARIETY STORE, GUYANA

Frank Bowling was the first son born to Agatha Elizabeth
Bowling on 26 February 1934 in a riverside town called
Bartica in Guyana, then known as British Guiana due to
colonisation. A businesswoman, she was a formidable figure
within the community; Bowling recalls that 'she ran the lives
of everybody'.[5] When the family relocated to the port town of
New Amsterdam in 1940, she established the first Bowling's
Variety Store on Pope Street, running a dressmaking and
millinery business alongside selling essential goods. She
eventually moved the flourishing enterprise to Main Street,
constructing a large three-storey house that became the family
home. This formative scene of Bowling's childhood later
became a signature part of his visual cartography: the shop
front is a recurring motif in his paintings (pp.31–5, 47), and

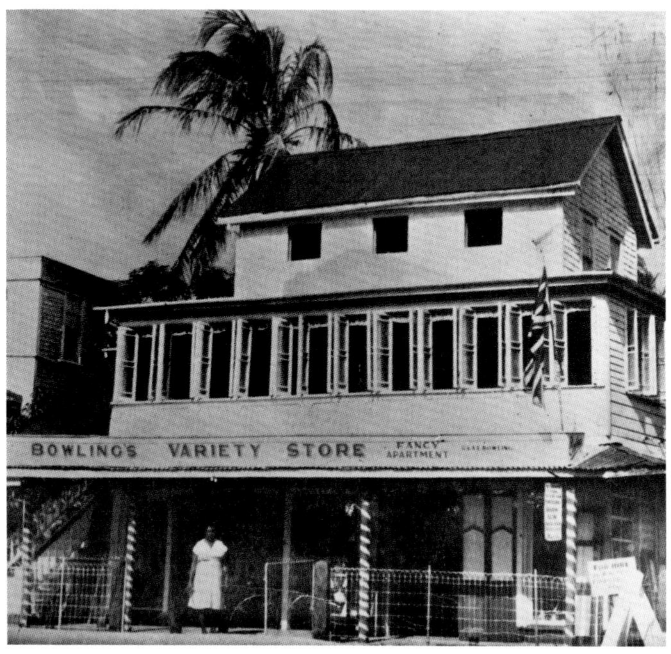

many are titled with a variation of *Mother's House* (pp.31–3, 40).
Indeed, Bowling has always attributed his impulse to create
to his mother, a maker: 'It is clear to me that making things is
influenced by my mother ... She had magic fingers, whatever
she touched.'[6] He remembers his role brushing mosquitos
away from her legs, so her sewing was not compromised as she
worked the treadle on her Singer machine; furthermore, his
canvases are textiles, her material.[7]

Guyana (meaning 'land of many waters'), on the North
Atlantic Ocean side of South America, is a mainland part
of what was called the British West Indies, which included
Jamaica, Barbados and Trinidad. The country shares a lot of
cultural history with both the Caribbean and South America.
Bartica means 'red earth' in one of the indigenous local
languages. The colour pink floods a series of Bowling's map
paintings called *Barticaborn* 1967–8 (pp.38–9), in which the
base colour of his first environment seems to have been a
starting point. The town sits between where two rivers join
the Essequibo, the largest river in Guyana. The confidence
with which Bowling commands deltas and rushes of liquid
colour could perhaps be attributed to the great rivers flowing

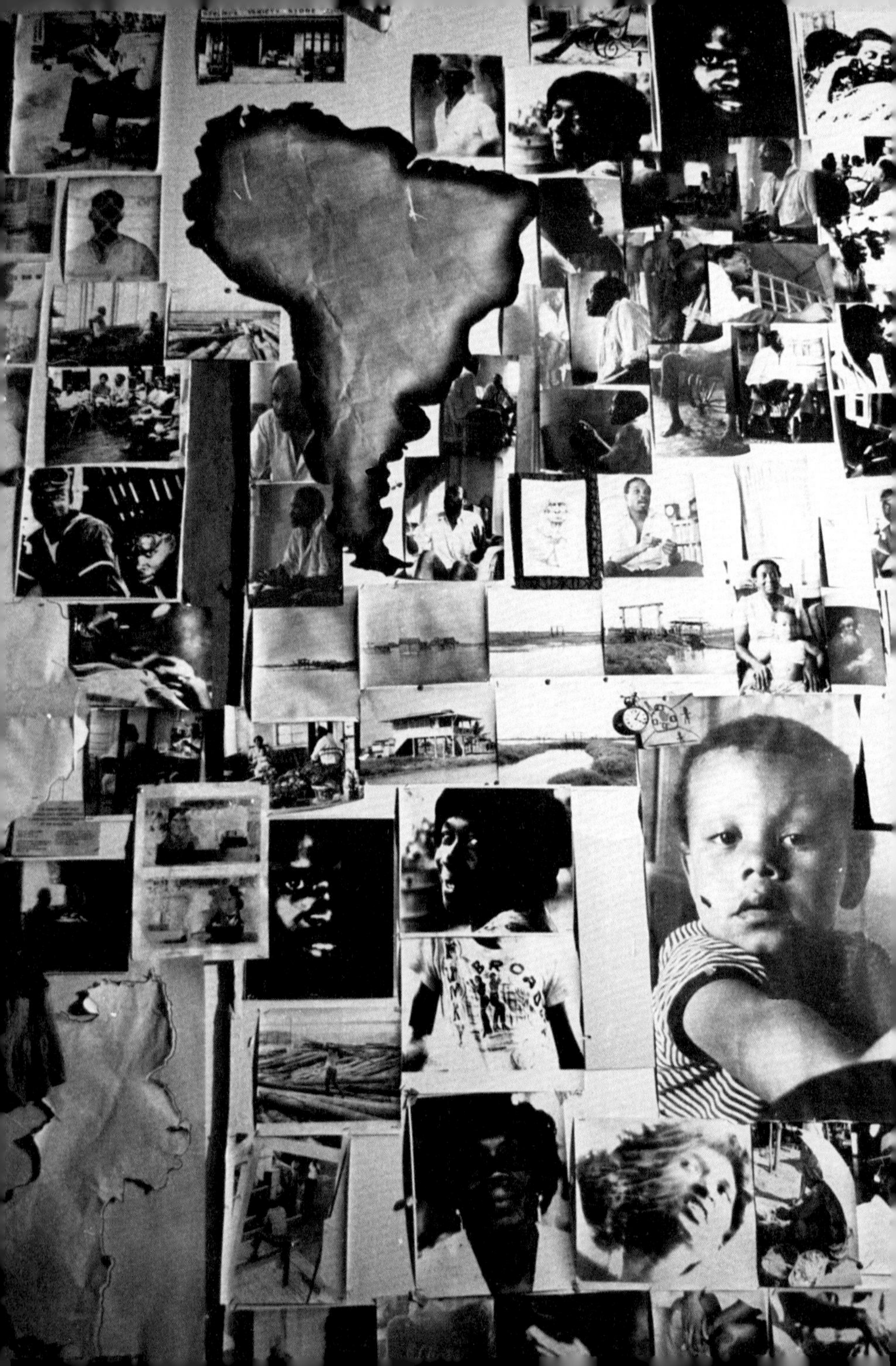

into the Atlantic Ocean. Bold reversal of flows can also be understood in response to violent history: Bartica has often been described as a 'gateway to the interior', because the rivers are used to take people back and forth from ocean to savannah and rainforest. Colonisers first met indigenous people on the river in the fifteenth century, and later used this route to reach their plantations (founded on enslaved labour) and gold and diamond mines – a reminder of how exploited the rich resources of the wider world were by Europeans.

New Amsterdam was the site of South America's first significant slave rebellion, the Berbice Slave Uprising of 1762–3.[8] Slavery was abolished in the British Caribbean in the 1830s. One hundred years on, Bowling grew up in a place deeply coloured by this period of industrial-scale inhumanity. He made two paintings titled *Middle Passage* in 1970 (pp.46–7). Family photographs and map stencils that were pinned to the wall of Bowling's Broadway studio in New York (opposite) are incorporated into both paintings within the red, gold and green of Pan-Africanism, obscured by layers of paint and blood-red seascapes. Art historian Dorothy Price has related the latter work to the 'inferno-filled sky' of the Old Testament in art: '*Middle Passage* serves as a secular altarpiece wherein the drowned bodies of the formerly enslaved become the ciphers for the lost martyrs and never-to-be-recovered saints … Standing in front of Bowling's monumental canvas calls for a meditative state of contemplation steeped in mourning and melancholia.'[9]

Bowling's father was authoritarian, regularly physically abusive, living in an almost silent bitterness. The artist Mel Gooding surmises that 'Bowling considers it an aspect of the violent inheritance of slavery', recalling 'so it was like trouble, trouble, trouble during my childhood', and he unsurprisingly rebelled at school, was beaten in response at home, and dreamed to 'just get out and go to London'.[10] He wanted adventure, perhaps seeded with some of his mother's determined example of how to create a successful life from scratch. Political consciousness of the moment of which he was part did not come at this point and, like so many young West Indians, he jumped at the call to help rebuild London after the Second World War. His father did not say goodbye. England may have been the 'mother country' but Bowling's early student portraits reckoned with masculinity (pp.10–11).

Images pinned to the wall of Frank Bowling's studio at 535 Broadway, SoHo, New York, c.1968. Photo: Daniel LaRue Johnson.

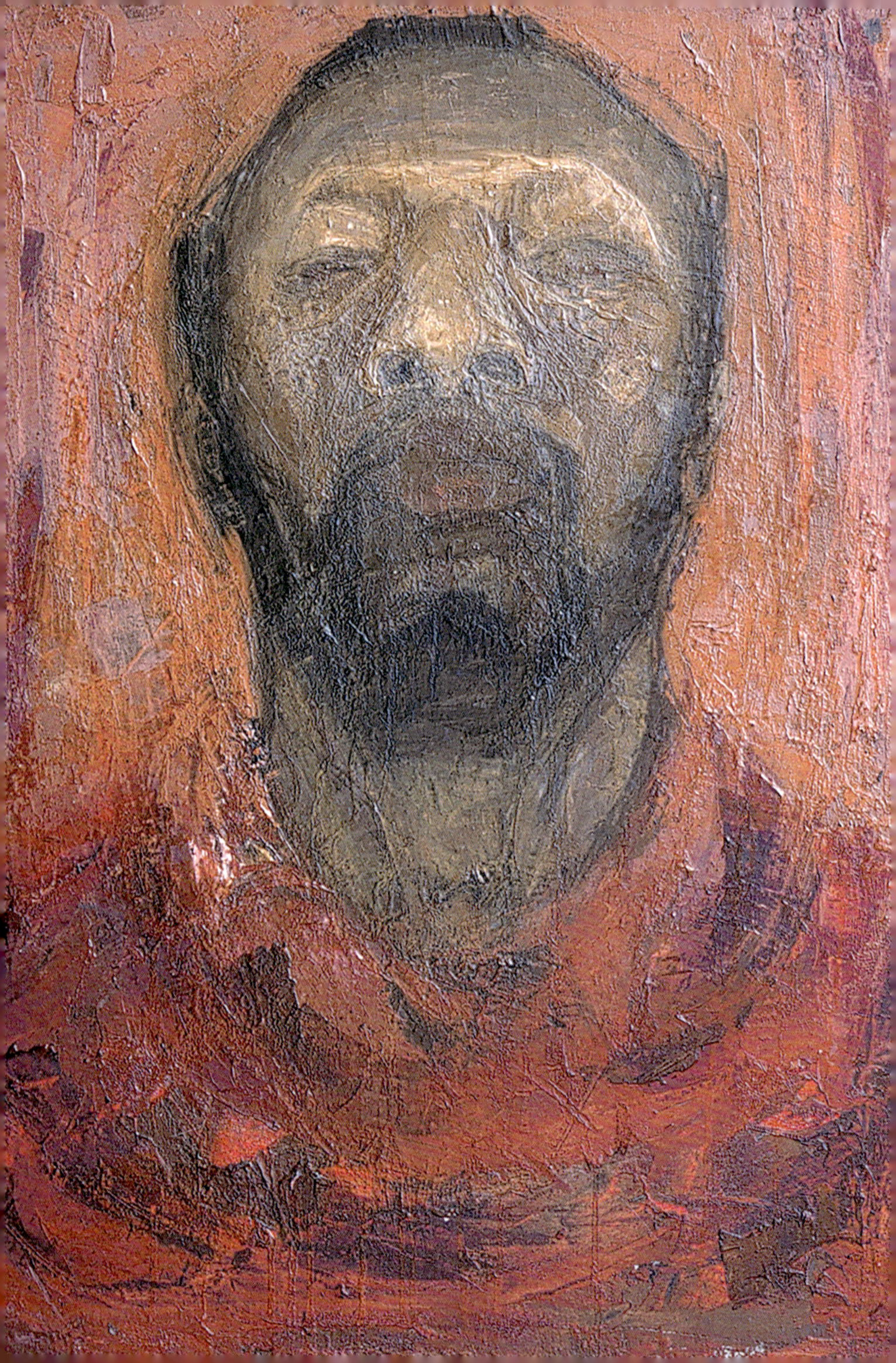

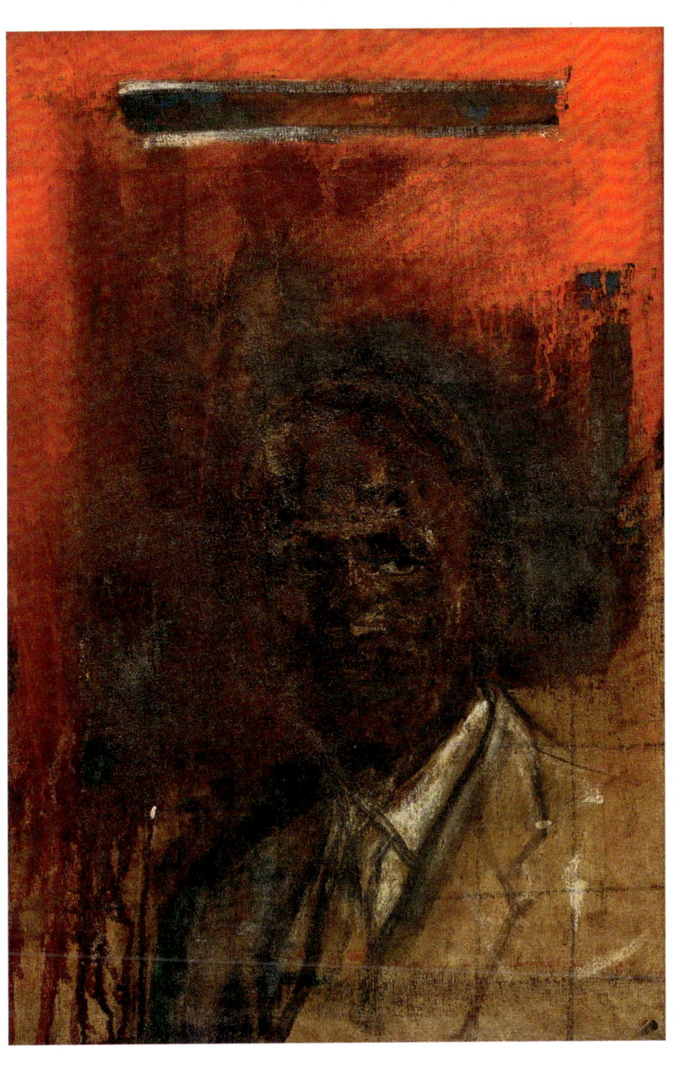

Self-Portrait 1959
Oil paint on canvas
91.5 × 61

Portrait of My Father 1960
Oil paint on canvas
84 × 58.5

The moment I arrived in London, I knew it was home.[11]

Bowling was only nineteen when he set off by boat to England in 1953. He was met at Waterloo station by his uncle Basil Franklin, and they travelled on by tube to North London amid the 'sheer energy of the heaving crowd' in 'coronation fever'.[12] When Queen Elizabeth II became Head of the Commonwealth, she gave a speech: 'Thus formed, the Commonwealth bears no resemblance to the Empires of the past. It is an entirely new conception … of an equal partnership of nations and races.'[13] There was a hope for new beginnings after the devastation of war. Labour was sought from the colonies – a hurried extraction as countries were gradually becoming independent – through posters and pamphlets enticing people to migrate. Contrary to the promise, they were met with racist hostility.

Despite the complex path through the harsh realities of exclusion, art offered a fresh start that suited the drive of a young man with a new life to form. Bowling's dying swan paintings of 1964 (pp.15, 28–9) suggest a decade of processing the contradictions of the bold new shapes and colours of a thrilling modern London still disrupted by the mighty beat of the wings of fading historic power.

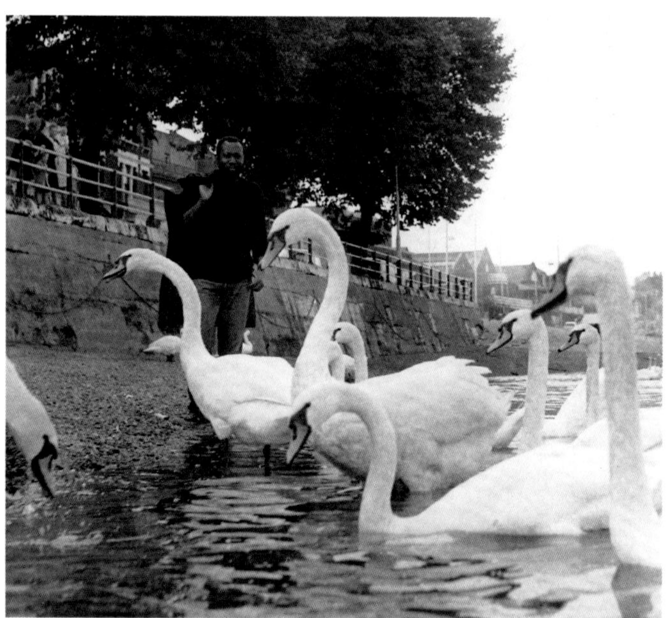

Black and white photograph of Frank Bowling standing behind a group of swans on the bank of the River Thames, c.1964, by Tina Tranter

Bowling had served in the Royal Air Force for nearly three unhappy years on first arrival in England. There, however, he met the artist Keith Critchlow, his 'first art teacher', who introduced him to the London art scene.[14] Bowling practised drawing and painting at evening classes, considered becoming a writer, worked on poetry, spent time in Paris, and struggled for money and a home while he explored what he might do with his life. He knew that his friend, the Irish painter Francis Bacon, was self-taught. Bacon's painting style influenced Bowling briefly as a student but perhaps the simultaneous artistic nonchalance and conviction that it was possible to make oneself into an artist was what was nurtured by the London scene in the longer term.

Carel Weight headed painting at the prestigious Royal College of Art (RCA) at the time that Bowling was employed to sit as a life model at the school. Weight encouraged him to paint and, after two attempts, he eventually attended through a scholarship. He was expelled for one term in 1960 because of his marriage to a staff member, Paddy Kitchen (but returned after she had moved jobs). In January 1962 Frank's first son Dan was born to Kitchen; in November of the same year, his second son Benjamin was born to the artist Claire Spencer; his third son Sacha was born in 1964 to Irene Delderfield. Photographs of Bowling and Kitchen on the spiral staircase of the RCA were a beginning for Bowling's celebrated painting *Mirror* 1964–6 (p.30), affirming the rich and playful crash course of influences the college afforded. Yet the *Beggar No 1 & 2* 1963 (p.27) diptych and other paintings from that period process fear and the violence of destitution, perhaps signalling the trauma of his precarious journey to this point.

ATLANTIC SWING

Once out of art school, Bowling found that the paths to success as an artist were thorny. A 'double consciousness' was necessary, an idea Paul Gilroy uses to describe the difficulties of being European and Black.[15] Bowling was not included in shows such as *54/64 Painting and Sculpture of a Decade* at Tate Gallery. At the same time, the succession of colonial independence stories on the front pages gave a visibility to artists and students from Commonwealth nations. In 1962, the Commonwealth Institute opened in Kensington in a new building, the architecture embodying the ideals of global interconnectedness.[16] Frank Bowling and Aubrey Williams

Cover of *Observer* magazine,
March 1966

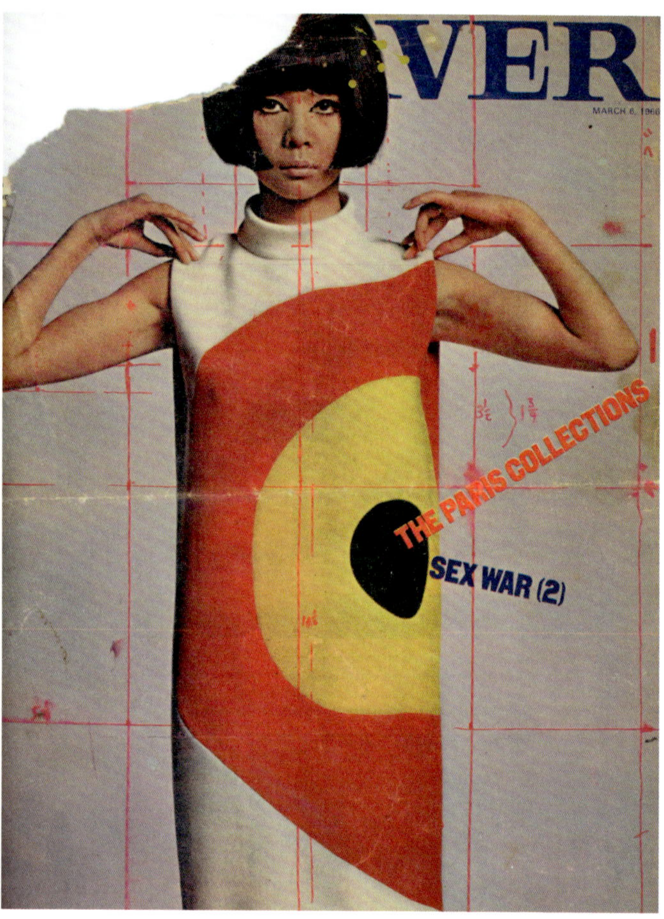

represented British Guiana in *Commonwealth Art Today*, the first
exhibition in the cross-cultural arts centre. Both artists had
lived an internationalism that was bigger than a conversation
between old Europe and new America.

In 1966, *Time* magazine popularised the phrase 'swinging
London' to describe the cultural and social revolution taking
place in the city. In *Cover Girl 1966* (p.34), Bowling used
an iconic London look from the cover of *Observer* magazine's
March 1966 issue (above) that was notably international:
Japanese model Hiroko Matsumoto wore the rounded bob
of London émigré hairdresser Vidal Sassoon and the pop
art principles of French-Italian Pierre Cardin's dress. *Untitled
(Mother's House)* (p.31), painted the same year, depicts the upper

body of a woman with the white dress and tied head of Black Creole cultures. Both figures foreground a screen-printed photograph of his mother's establishment taken around the time of the coronation, the same year Bowling left Guyana for England. Questions of belonging were not straightforward.

After graduating, Bowling transferred a scholarship offered to visit Rome to fund a trip to Guyana instead, where he travelled to New Amsterdam. He was constantly engaged in the swing and synthesis of influences; before he began literally tipping his canvases later in the 1970s, he was deftly tilting the direction of his sources. As he stated: 'I didn't want to have to go anywhere but stay in London and do my work, right? But I was curious to see the Caribbean ... There was an awful lot of attention being paid to the fact that I was born in the Caribbean, so I thought I should go and look at that ... I was in my element.'[17]

An ambivalent swing began to electrify his work. Some accounts suggest that Bowling was persuaded by artist Roland Penrose to represent Britain at the First World Festival of Negro Arts in Dakar, Senegal, in 1966 (the country had achieved independence from France in 1960). The host was the first president, Léopold Senghor, renowned for championing the cultural renaissance of African countries and their diasporas. Bowling was awarded the grand prize for contemporary art for the painting that culminated the dying swan trio: *Big Bird* 1964 (below).[18]

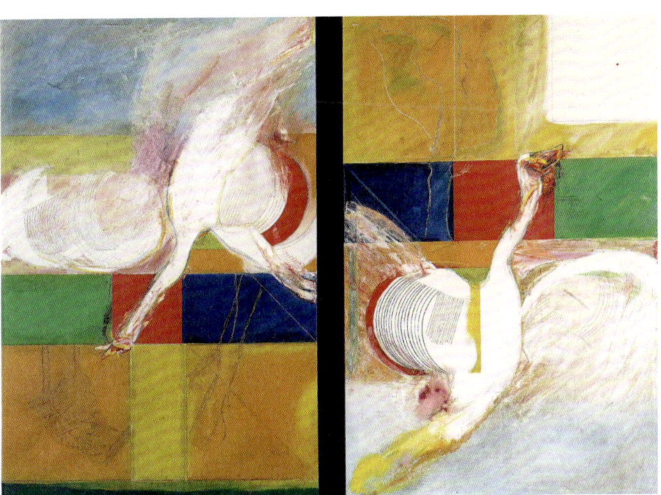

Big Bird 1964
Oil paint and velvet fabric
on canvas
183 × 259

An Atlantic triangulation began.[19] Fully locating to New York in 1966, Bowling frequently stayed at the renowned Chelsea Hotel, before moving to his first studio on Beekman Street. At the beginning of 1967, winning a Guggenheim Fellowship meant he could move from a single-room studio to a larger loft space on Broadway, where he lived and worked until 1975. A step up in scale was possible, and map paintings became a sustained focus.

In 1968, two years after Guyana gained independence, Bowling visited New Amsterdam again – this time with his friend, British photographer Tina Tranter, to document people and places from his youth. He created silk screens from Tranter's photographs and went on to use them alongside previously made silk screens in paintings, including *Bartica 1968–9*, and map stencils in *Where is Lucienne?* 1971 (p.54).

In 1969, Bowling made a notable debut with *Dan Johnson's Surprise* in the Whitney Annual at the Whitney Museum of American Art, which showcased his innovative approach to abstraction and solidified his reputation among contemporary artists in the US. This momentum culminated in 1971 when he received his first solo exhibition at the Whitney. That year, he featured again in their group exhibition *Contemporary Black Artists in America*. The latter also affirmed his role as a significant figure in the dialogue surrounding race and identity. He wrestled for this to be on his own terms, about

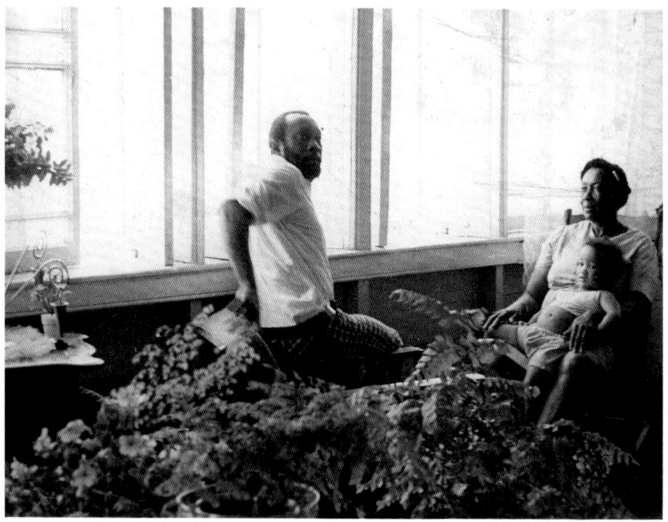

Black and white photograph of Frank Bowling, his mother and his nephew Francis in New Amsterdam, 1968, by Tina Tranter

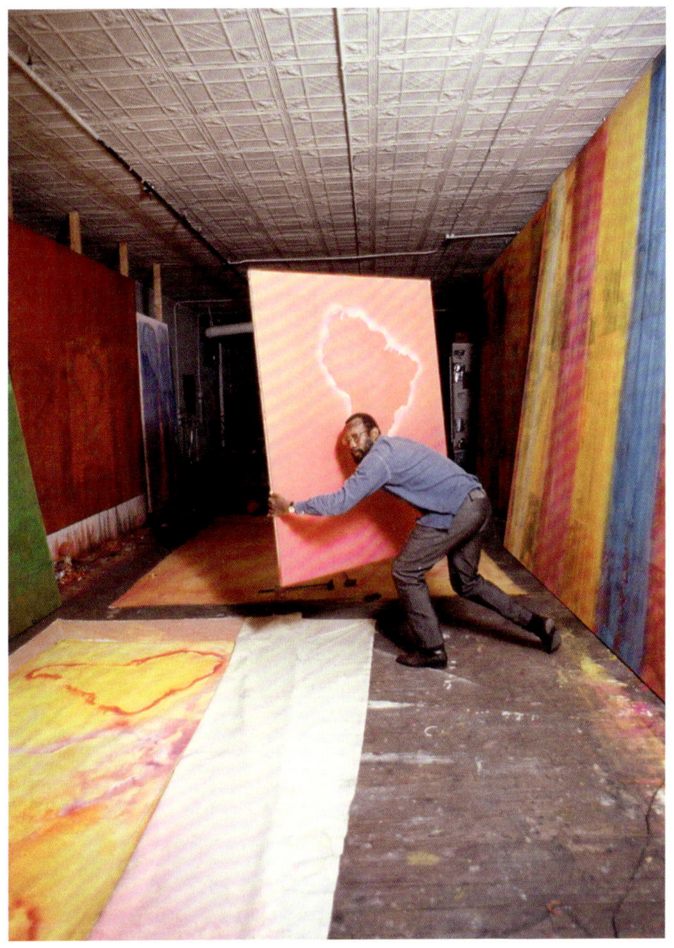

his work not about his ethnicity, without compromising his
solidarity with fellow Black artists.

In commitment to shared culture, identity and experience,
he curated the exhibition 5+1 at the Art Gallery of the State
University of New York in 1969. It showed the remarkable
works of five leading Black American artists – Melvin Edwards,
Al Loving, Jack Whitten, Daniel LaRue Johnson and William
T. Williams – alongside Bowling's own contributions. In the
accompanying pamphlet, Bowling wrote '10 Notes From
a Work in Progress', in which he reflected on creative process:
'From masks to funeral jazz, from politically subversive
spirituals to the work of present Black artists and writers,

17

the relationship between aesthetics and reality is binding, deliberate, and harmonious.'[20]

In 1969–70, Bowling published three connected articles in *Arts Magazine* addressing the intense debate around 'Black art' in the United States. He resisted the idea that Black art must be purely political. In his first article, Bowling discusses the importance of valuing Black art within the broader context of contemporary art; the second critiques the narratives that often marginalise Black artists, advocating for a more inclusive approach; in the third, he reflects further on the role of identity in art, exploring how personal and cultural histories shape the work of Black artists and revolutionise the larger art discourse.[21] In his essay for the book *Black Life and Culture in the United States*, published in 1971, he asks 'Is Black Art About Color?' and concludes: 'Are Black people missing many links, in dealing with modernism? Since a prevailing aesthetic expression in paint is completely identified with whites, the honest answer is that were we not afraid in many ways of being considered white, we would be truly Black.'[22]

The painting *Who's Afraid of Barney Newman* 1968 (p.41) makes informal reference to a key figure in American abstract expressionism, Barnett Newman. Like Newman's 1966–70 series *Who's Afraid of Red, Yellow and Blue* (the primary colours affirming that colour can be everything), Bowling's title is not punctuated with a question mark: it is a statement staking a claim to abstract work. Yet, as Price writes about Bowling as a landscape artist, his depiction of continents devastated by the violence of colonialism commands a sublime possibility for art to reckon with questions beyond the canvas.[23] Bowling replaces Newman's primary colours with stencilled continental maps cut with the red, green and gold of Rastafarianism, and eventually the flags of multiple African countries.

NEW YORK & JUST PAINTING

It took until 1971 or 1972 to convince me to make a direct statement – just to paint … having been preoccupied all my life with the socio-political problem of being a Black person.[24]

In 1970, Bowling met the influential critic Clement Greenberg, known for his writing on American modern art. They began a long friendship and correspondence,[25] during which Bowling entered a period of energetic 'colour field' painting, without any representation of the world beyond the painted surface.

Caesar's Plume 1975
Acrylic paint on canvas
167 × 84

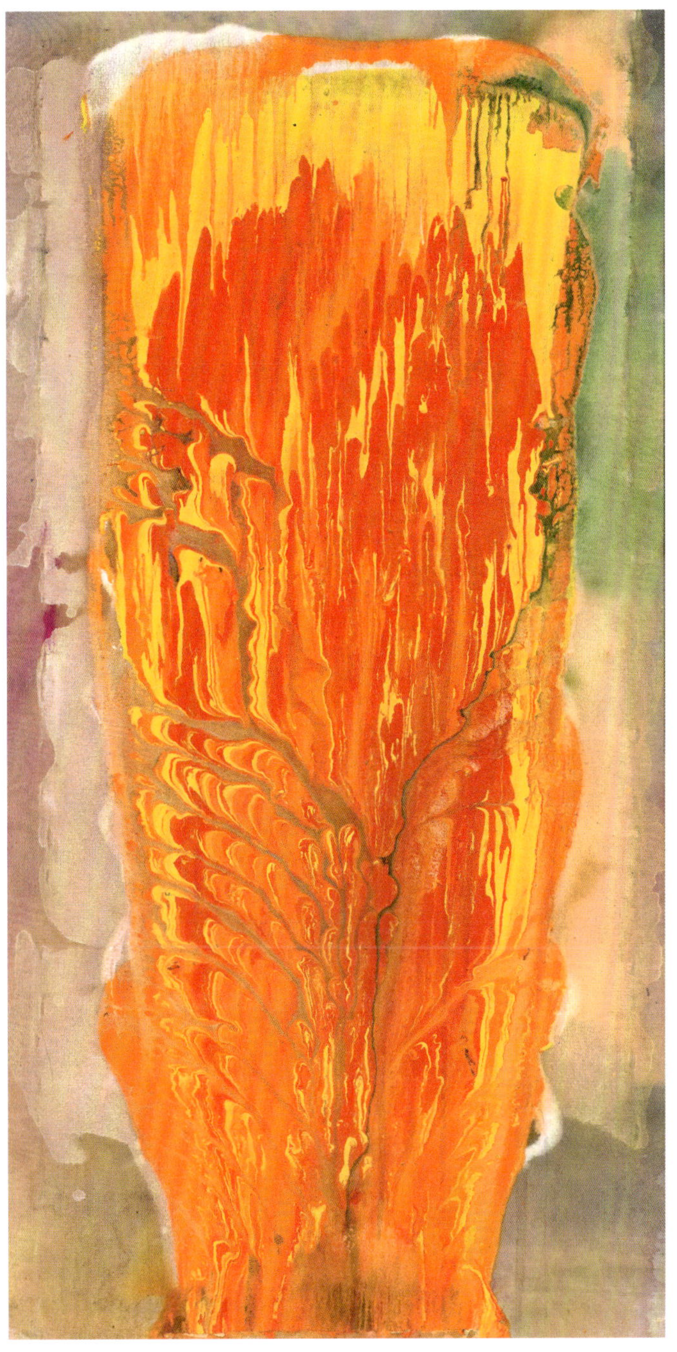

Greenberg associated this style with Helen Frankenthaler and other New York artists innovating 'post-painterly abstraction', as he described this second wave of abstract expressionism with its fresh techniques, lyricism and clarity.

In 1973, Bowling built a tilting platform to pour paint directly onto his canvases from above head height. Canvases were tacked to the platform, and different thicknesses and quantities of paint ran down the surfaces in varied directions. These controlled experiments with chance created poured paintings, including *Ziff* 1974 (p.67), *Caesar's Plume* 1975 (p.19) and *Tony's Anvil* 1975 (p.71). Bowling eventually began to look further than the automatic making of the poured paintings, which had initially allowed him to explore spontaneity and fluidity in his work. The approach was never abandoned, but Bowling started to incorporate more intention and complexity into his compositions through new methods and materials, ultimately leading to a more nuanced incorporation of identity and culture.

LONDON'S 'MOVE, DRIP, CASCADE & SLITHER'

The fact is, it's exciting and challenging to work in London, Turner's town, and the pressures of the weight of the British tradition are exhilarating.[26]

Though New York was, and still is, an important home for Bowling's studio practice, the 1980s were mostly spent in the proximity of London's River Thames. Home and studio moved between Pimlico, Cable Street (East End) and Elephant and Castle, all evoking an older, working city: gritty, wet and layered with history, as felt in the paintings *Wintergreens* 1986 (p.83), *Great Thames II* 1989 (p.82) and *Kitty* 2009 (pp.84–5). Remembering a 1989 Arts Council studio visit (which resulted in the acquisition of a work from the *Great Thames* series), the artist Sonia Boyce described the impact of the paintings: 'Engulfed in the presence of these monumental works up close in his studio, their sheer physicality overwhelmed me. Thick layers of paint trowelled across a huge expanse of canvas, yet with a pearlescent surface.'[27]

In this reinterpretation of the English landscape tradition, the surfaces of Bowling's canvases were heavily loaded with the thick light and textures of England, rather than realistic depictions. The canvas became a three-dimensional landscape with slower, encrusted paint joining floods of colour, while assorted objects slowly found their eventual drying position within acrylic gels.[28] In 1983 Bowling settled in his current flat in Pimlico, near to Tate Gallery, home of the Turner Bequest. This comprises more than 30,000 paintings, drawings and sketches by J.M.W. Turner, demonstrating his profound influence on modern art through the drama and deft control of paint, colour and light. Bowling responded with sublime shafts of light on water, but also the domesticity of a small island now shed of most of its empire. Working from a view of the New Forest from a Hampshire hotel window, he further observed: 'if you go directly at that kind of thing you can end up with chocolate box art. But now I feel I can accommodate it, as it were, without giving it away or losing it. In the hotel you get a free little packet of sewing stuff, and I put the contents of that packet in the painting.'[29]

The late 1980s saw a period of metal sculpting using salvaged elements (below), tipping the interplay between flat and three-dimensional forms away from painting. Curator Sam Cornish noted that geometry was a tool Bowling used as a practical means to 'incorporate rigour into a broadly instinctive

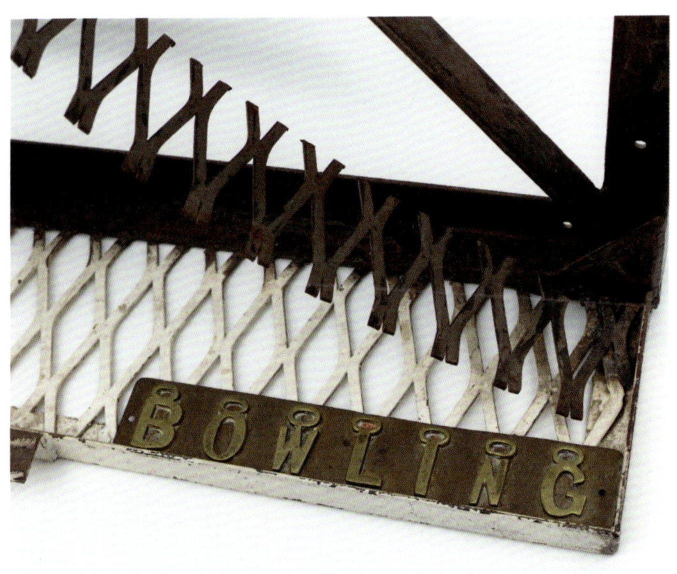

Angharad's Gift Patagonia
(detail) 1991
Welded steel
92 × 94 × 34

approach to making'. Recounting a teenage apprenticeship with an uncle who was a cabinetmaker in Guyana, Bowling learned 'how triangles and circles would fit within squares to make rock-solid furniture'.[30] The spirals, grilles and angles of these works take us back to the spiral stairs at the RCA, and further back to Bowling's Variety Store and a verandah life populated with stands for lush vegetation. The geometry is furniture for feeling and memory.

Debate about Black art was flourishing in England. Sonia Boyce has noted that, though she and Bowling both attended the iconic First National Black Art Convention in Wolverhampton in 1982, she was then unaware of his presence and significance.[31] She took notice when *The Other Story*, the groundbreaking exhibition curated by artist Rasheed Araeen for London's Hayward Gallery in 1989–90, showed work by Bowling. The focus was the contributions of Black and Asian artists to British art, challenging the Eurocentric narratives of the time. It was a vital catalyst for broader recognition and inclusion of marginalised talents in the art world, paving the way for the ongoing rectification of representation in contemporary art institutions. Bowling had fought hard for recognition on the basis of his work alone, so had to be persuaded to be included.[32]

Nonetheless, his work continued to show his ties to Guyana. The painting *SachaJasonGuyanaDreams* 1989 marks a shift in attitude to Guyana. Bowling and his son Sacha travelled there together, and Sacha affirmed that he recognised something from the use of colour and light in his father's paintings in the country he was experiencing for the first time. In the 1990s Frank met the Guyanese photographer and writer Spencer Richards, further increasing his openness to considering cultural heritage.[33]

TWENTY-FIRST CENTURY BITTER SWEET

In 2001, the devastating loss of Bowling's first son Dan led to a series of white paintings. These recalled the snow that had settled outside when Bowling awaited his son's birth in 1962 (when he had painted two winter landscapes).[34]

The twenty-first century brought late recognition in the art world, which has been the experience of many of the most important Black artists who are part of shaping modern and contemporary art. Bowling made history in 2005 by becoming the first Black artist to be elected to the Royal Academy for his outstanding contribution to the visual arts – a striking milestone, considering the 200-year history of the institution, which underscores the slow change of the art community. In 2008, Bowling was awarded an OBE (Order of the British Empire) and expressed mixed feelings about accepting the honour. This continued a career-long tension between recognition for extraordinary achievement and a system of categorisation and oppression of Black excellence.

In 2012, *Drop, Roll, Slide, Drip... Frank Bowling's Poured Paintings 1973–8* opened at Tate Britain, with *Mappa Mundi* following in 2017 in Munich. The latter was Bowling's first international touring show, travelling on to Dublin and the UAE – places deeply invested in decolonial debate. That same year, Bowling was the only non-North American featured in *Soul of a Nation: Art in the Age of Black Power* at Tate Modern, an exhibition that toured across the United States, affirming the ongoing relationship to the transatlantic narrative of Black art and culture.

In 2019, Bowling's first major survey exhibition opened at Tate Britain, the celebration with which this book began. He received a knighthood in 2020. Many artists whose work explores the breathtaking possibilities of paint and profoundly responds to British Atlantic diasporic experience cite Bowling as an influence, from Hurvin Anderson and Lynette Yiadom-Boakye to Oscar Murillo and Rachel Jones. In 2022, the British sculptor Thomas J. Price reflected: 'I think as a Black artist whose pioneering career has spanned so many decades of social change, and who refused to have his output dictated by the expectations of white society, it's very hard to not recognise a political power in Frank's work.'[35]

I was born between two rivers. Pisces. All there was was fish. [36]

'LILTING OF WATER & OTHER MATERIAL'

The year 2025 marked a return to maps, to stories of Bowling's beginnings. The artist Ben Gooding remade the stencil of South America at Camberwell College of Arts, where Bowling first made them in a textiles studio.[37] The originals have become archival objects, but the working versions faithfully replicate Bowling's particular mapping of the continent outline. During a studio visit in early 2025, Bowling pointed out that a stencil of Guyana was tucked horizontally into the bars on the window, sideways, 'the way it is seen by the gold diggers

– Raleigh!' (opposite).[38] He remembered that, as a schoolboy, he was shamed for not being able to draw Guyana perfectly from memory. New paintings lined the studio walls, each marked with São Paulo, the only city named in the South America stencil, and one painting returned to the continent for the Bienal de São Paulo in September 2025.

Bowling paints daily in his Peacock Yard studio in London. His son Ben and grandson Frederik are often there; a chair is upholstered with a knitted cover by Rachel. Buckets of paint sit on a murky canvas in an inch of liquid on the floor, leaving their unpredictable mark, while strips of fluorescent canvas wait in a basket to be stitched on. Crusts, pools, rivers, oceans of colour illuminate every corner of this world.

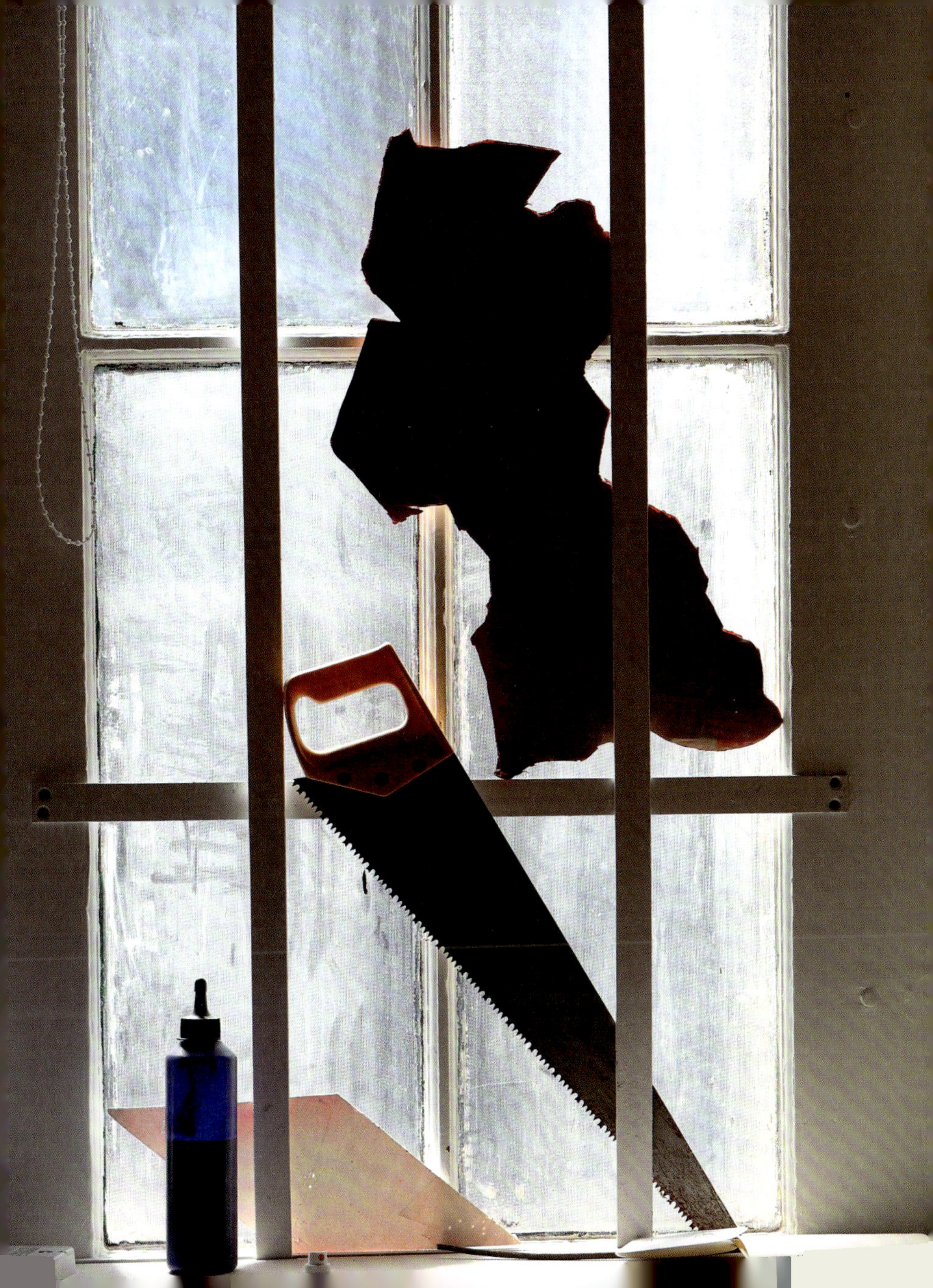

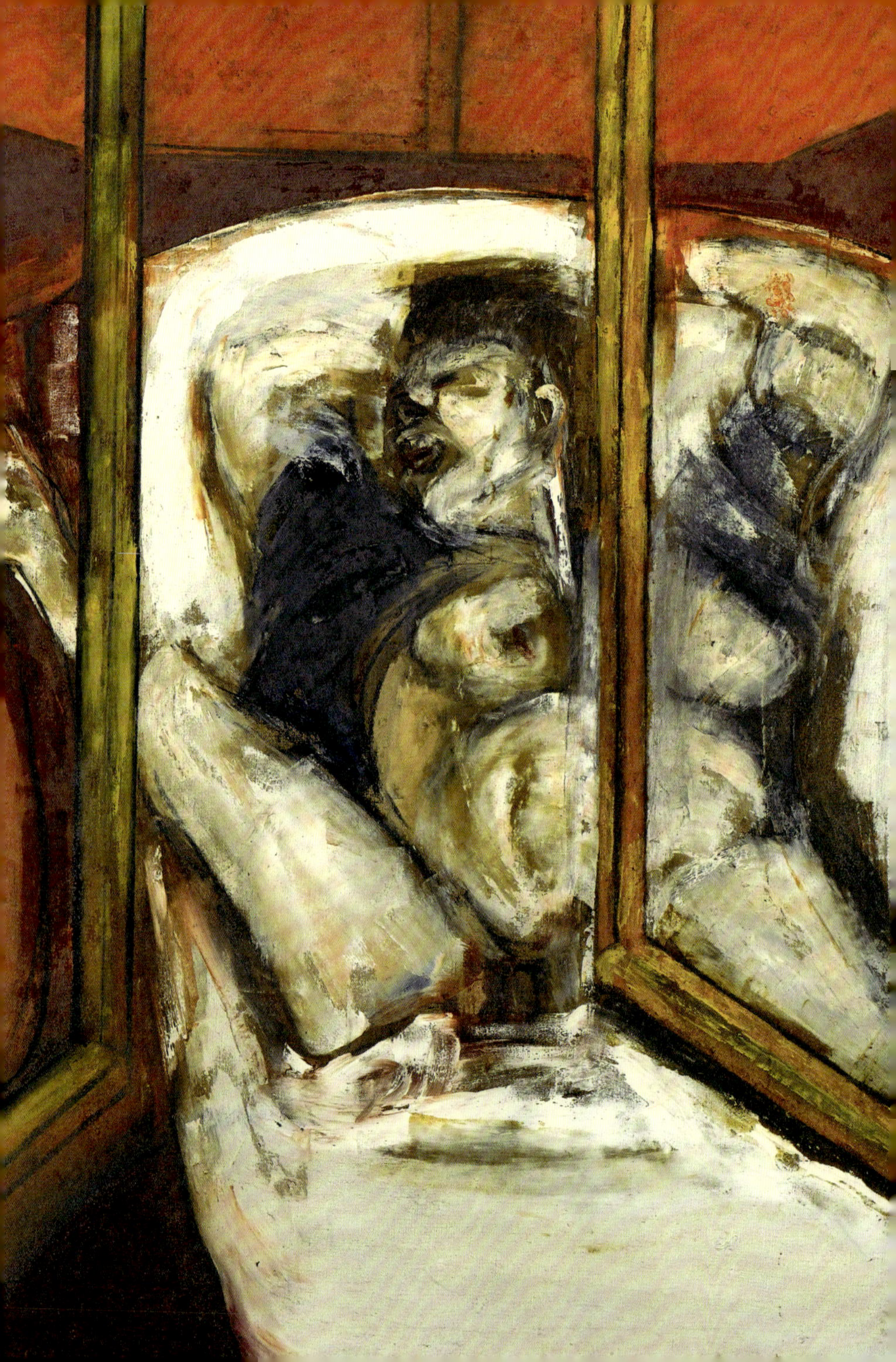

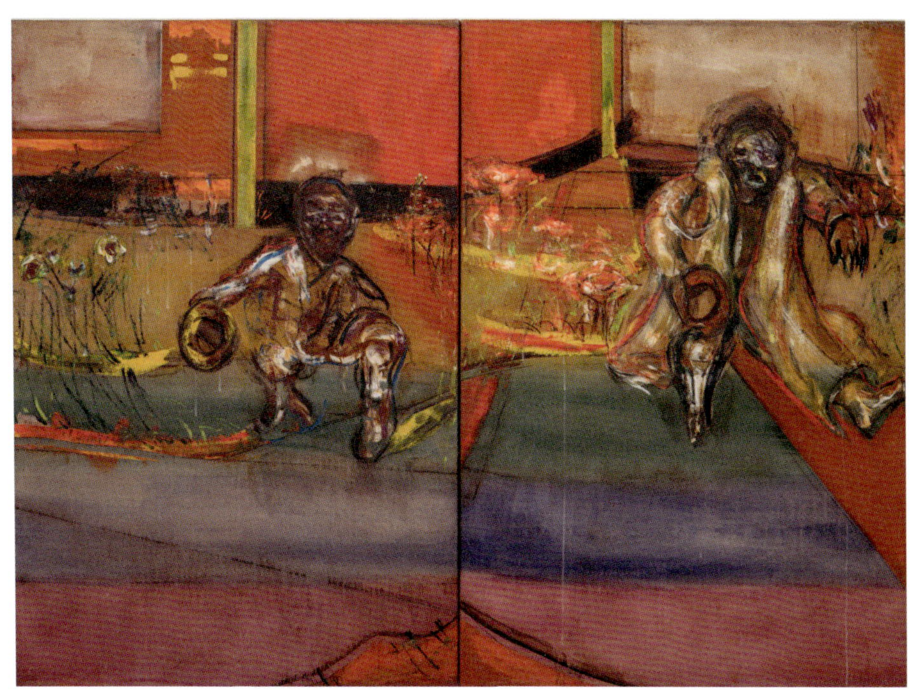

Birthday 1962
Oil paint on canvas
121.9 × 91.4

Beggar No.1 & 2 1963
Oil paint on canvas
101.6 × 147.3

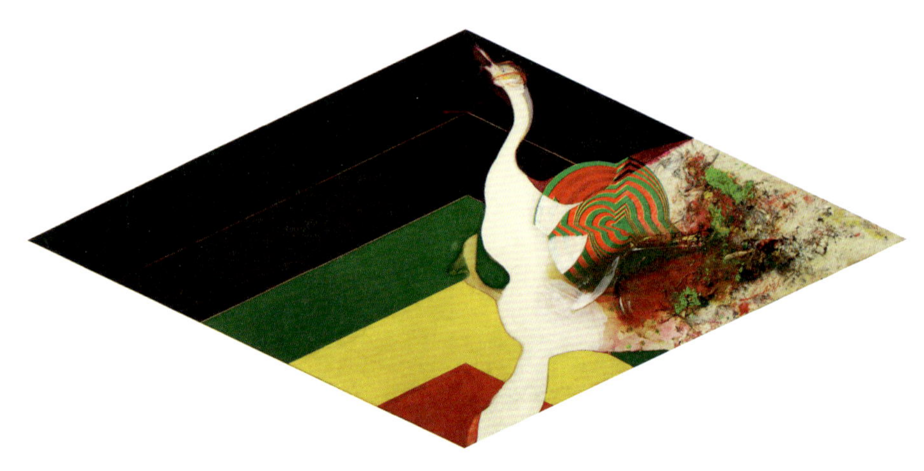

Swan I 1964
Oil paint and feathers on
canvas
112 × 244

Swan II 1964
Oil paint on canvas
112 × 243

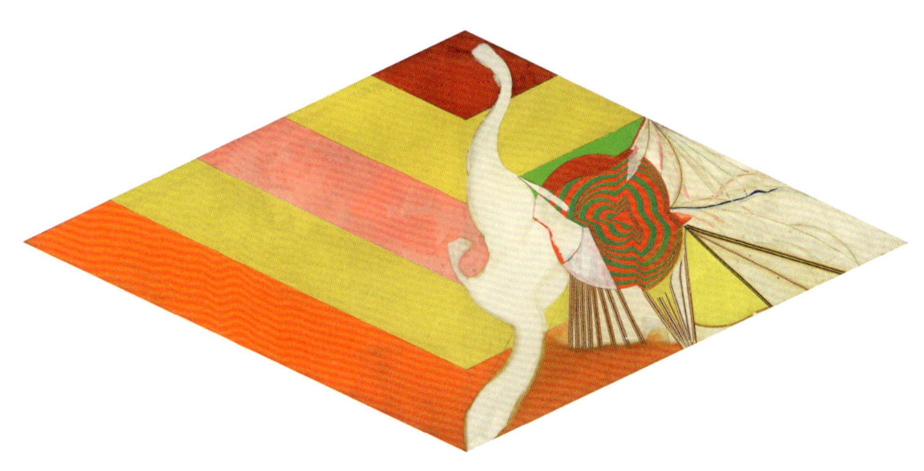

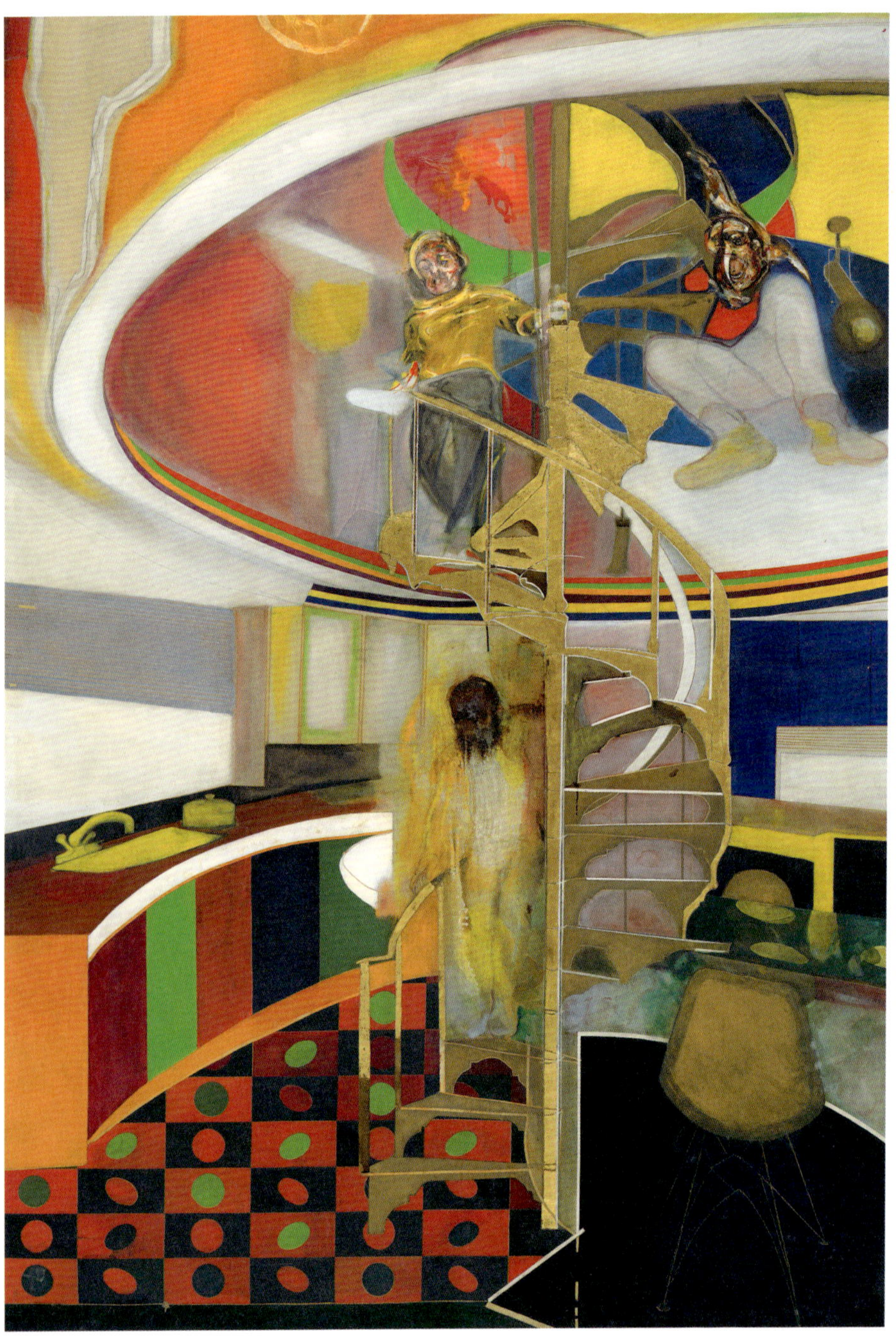

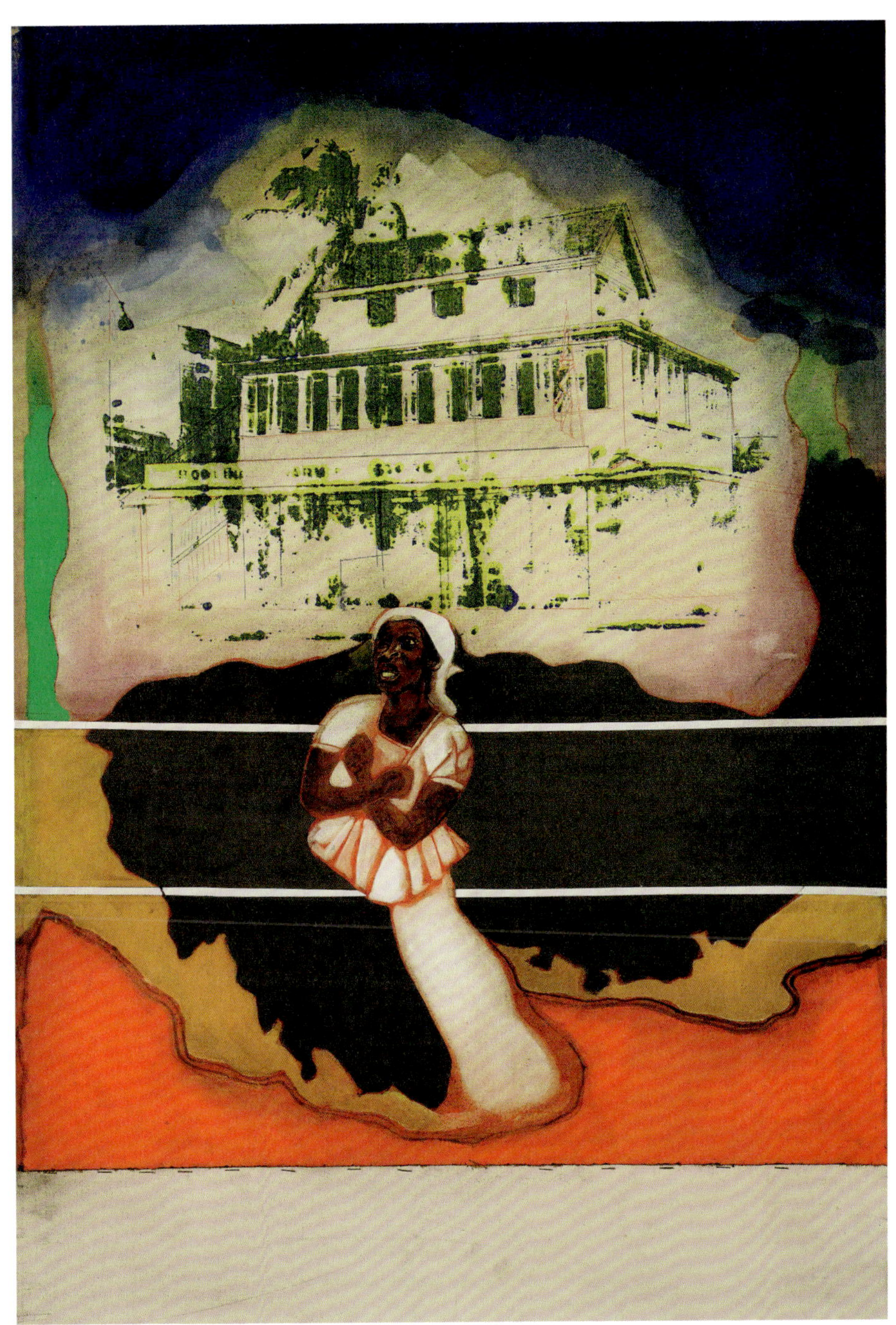

*Palimpsest 1 – Mother's House
DarkRedGreen 1966*
Acrylic paint and
silkscreened ink on canvas
62.5 × 172.5

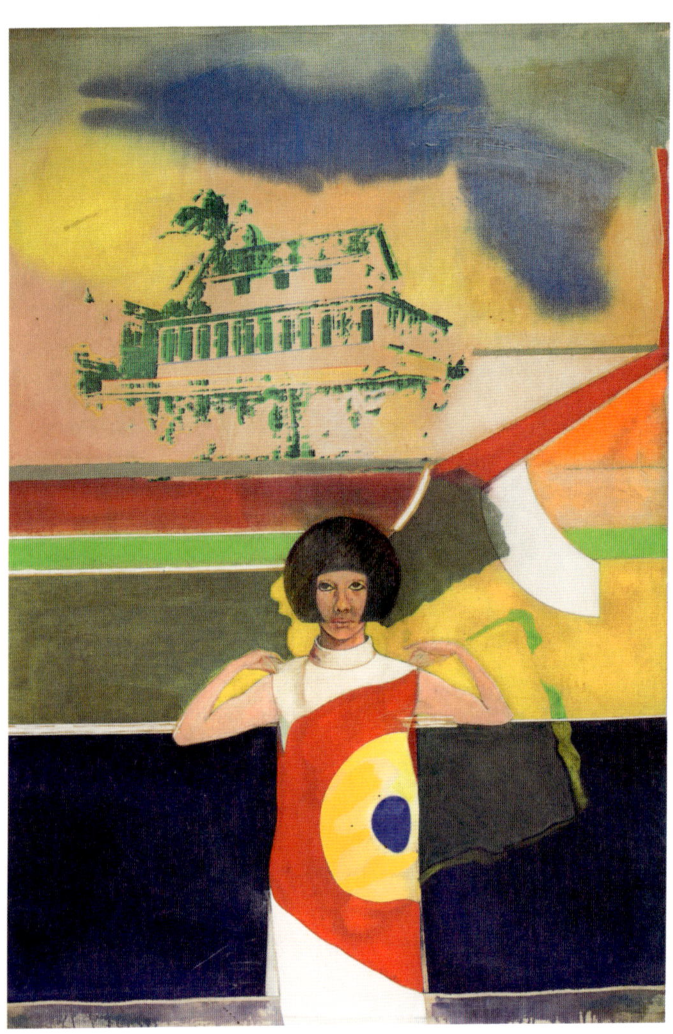

Cover Girl 1966
Acrylic paint, oil paint and
silkscreened ink on canvas
149.8 × 101.6

Barticabather 1966–7
Mixed media on collaged
canvas
148 × 102

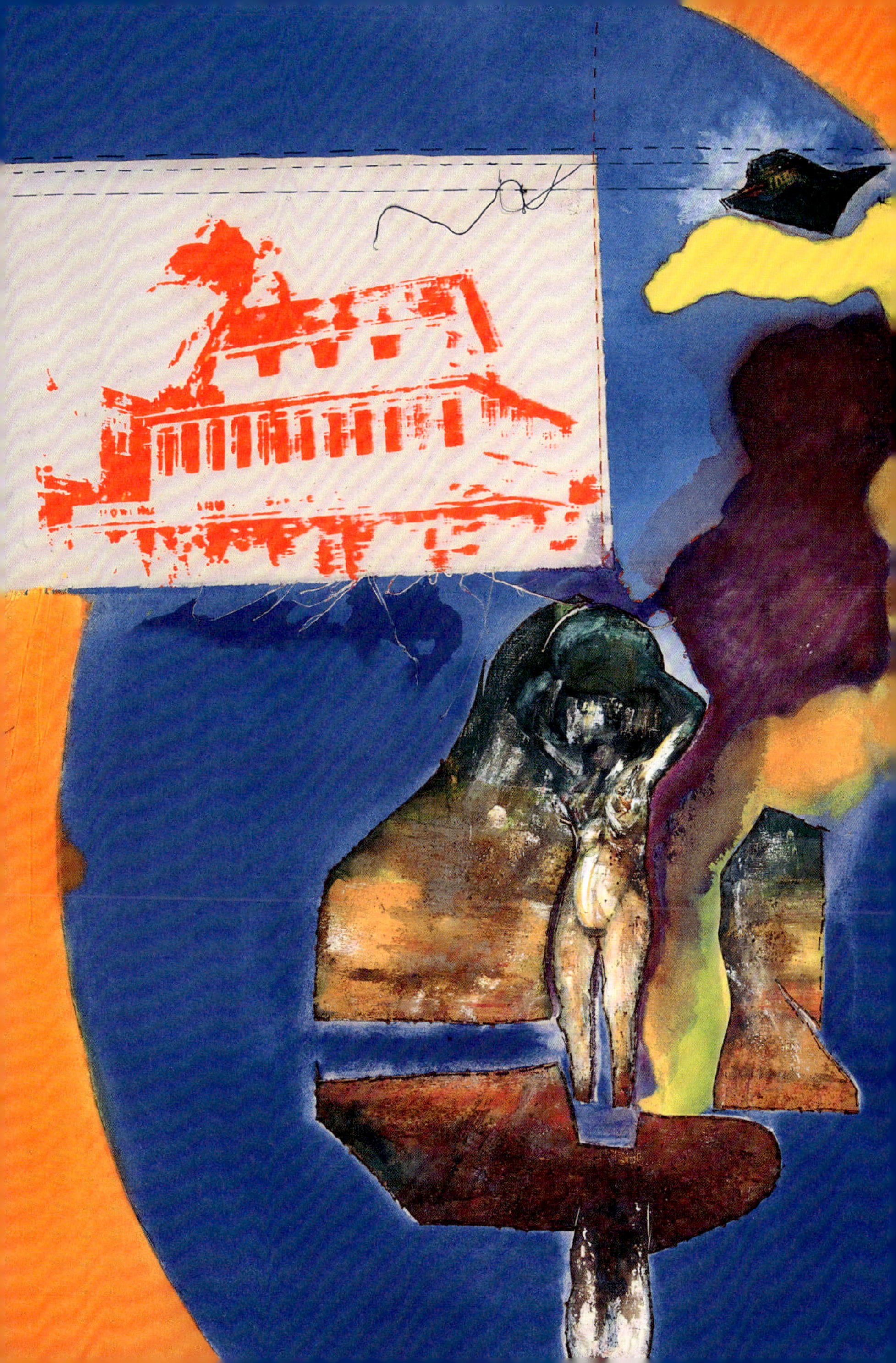

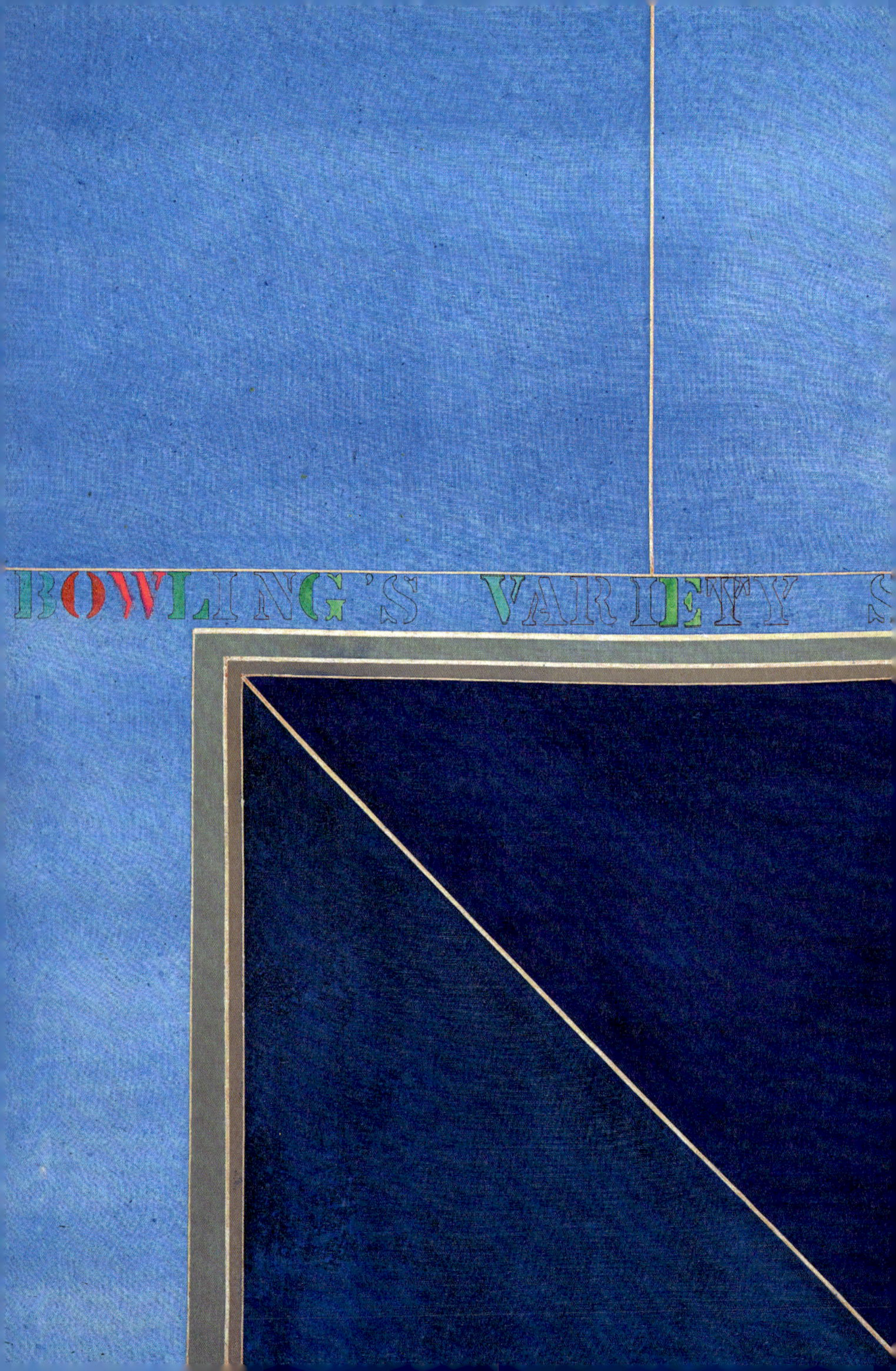

BOWLING'S VARIETY S

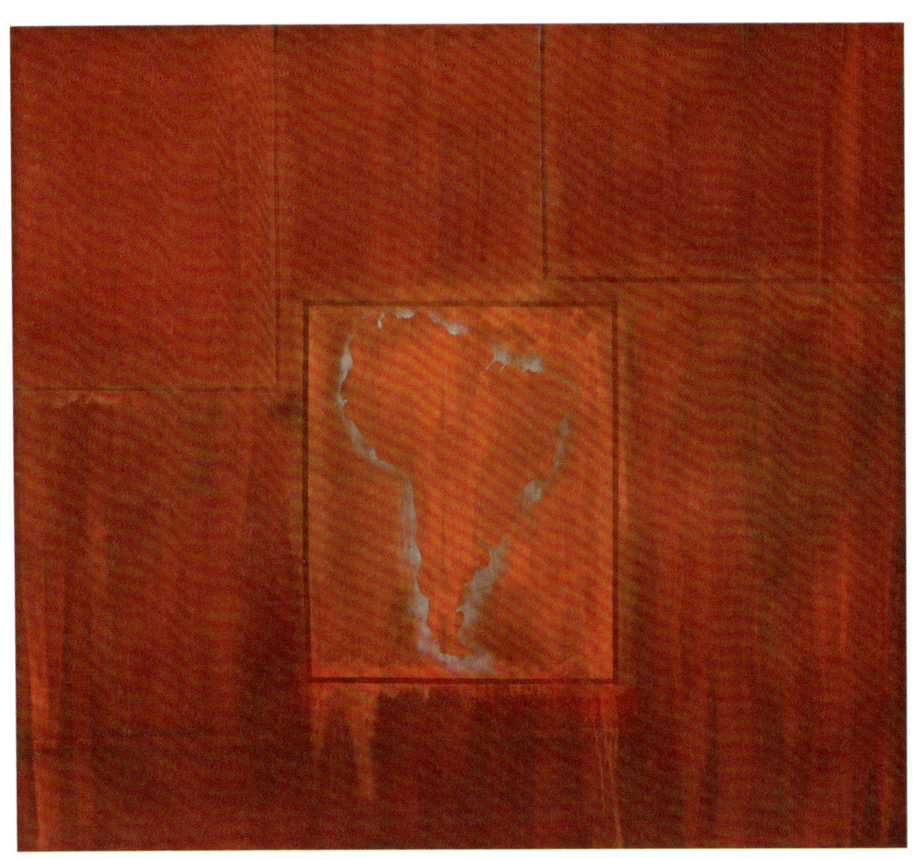

Bowling's Variety Store 1967
Acrylic paint on canvas
120.5 × 79

South America Squared 1967
Acrylic paint and spray
paint on canvas
243 × 274

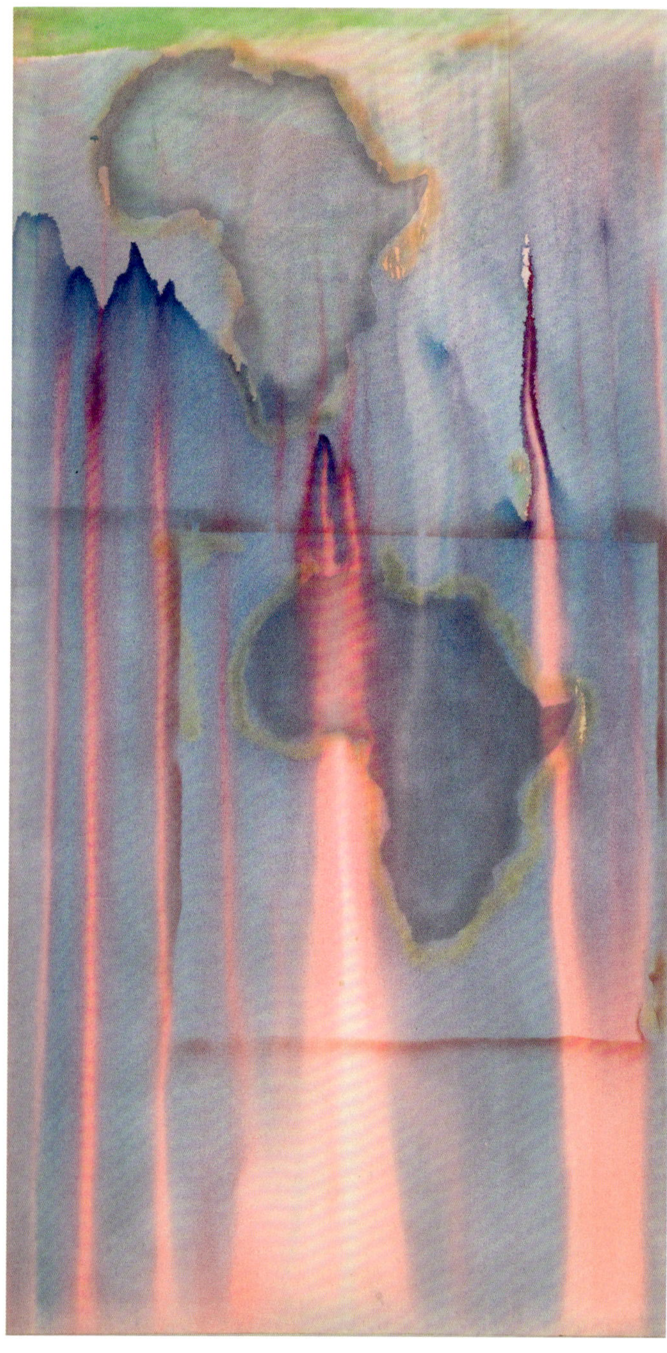

Barticaborn I 1967
Acrylic paint, spray paint
and oil wax on canvas
234 × 122.4

Barticaborn III 1968
Acrylic paint on canvas
289 × 140

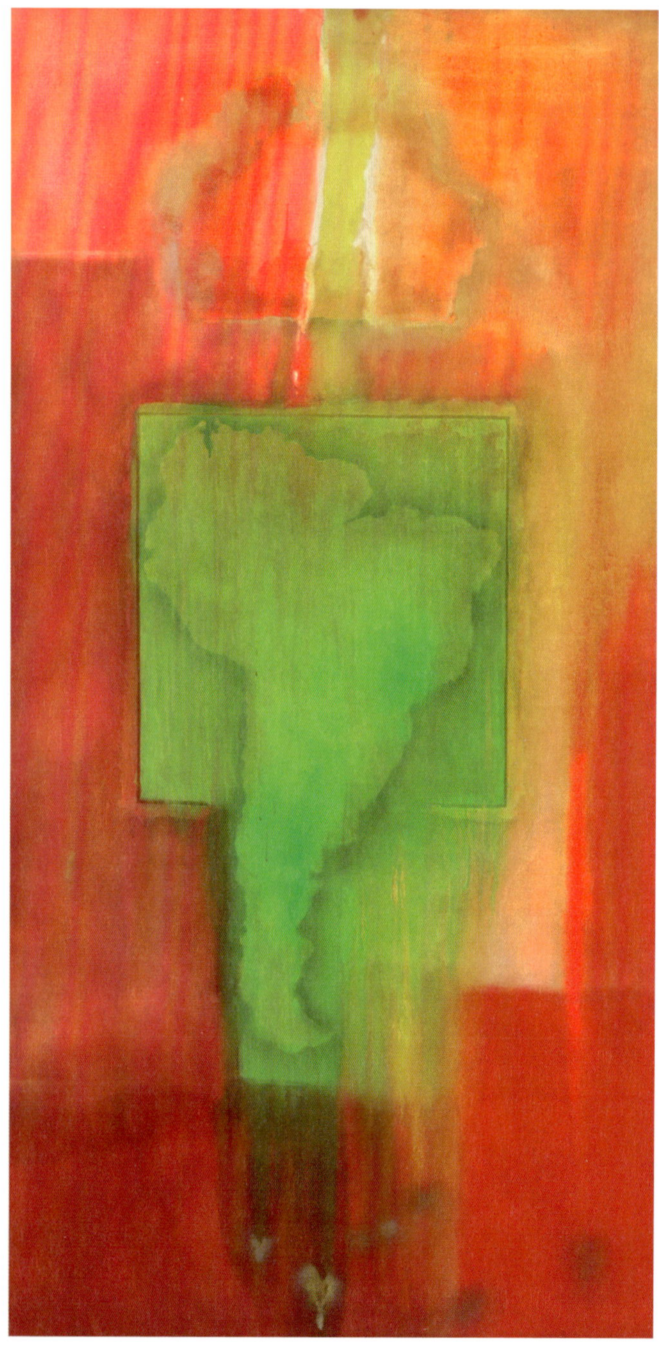

Mother's House on South
America 1968
Acrylic paint on canvas
233.6 × 121.9

Who's Afraid of Barney
Newman 1968
Acrylic paint on canvas
236.4 × 129.5

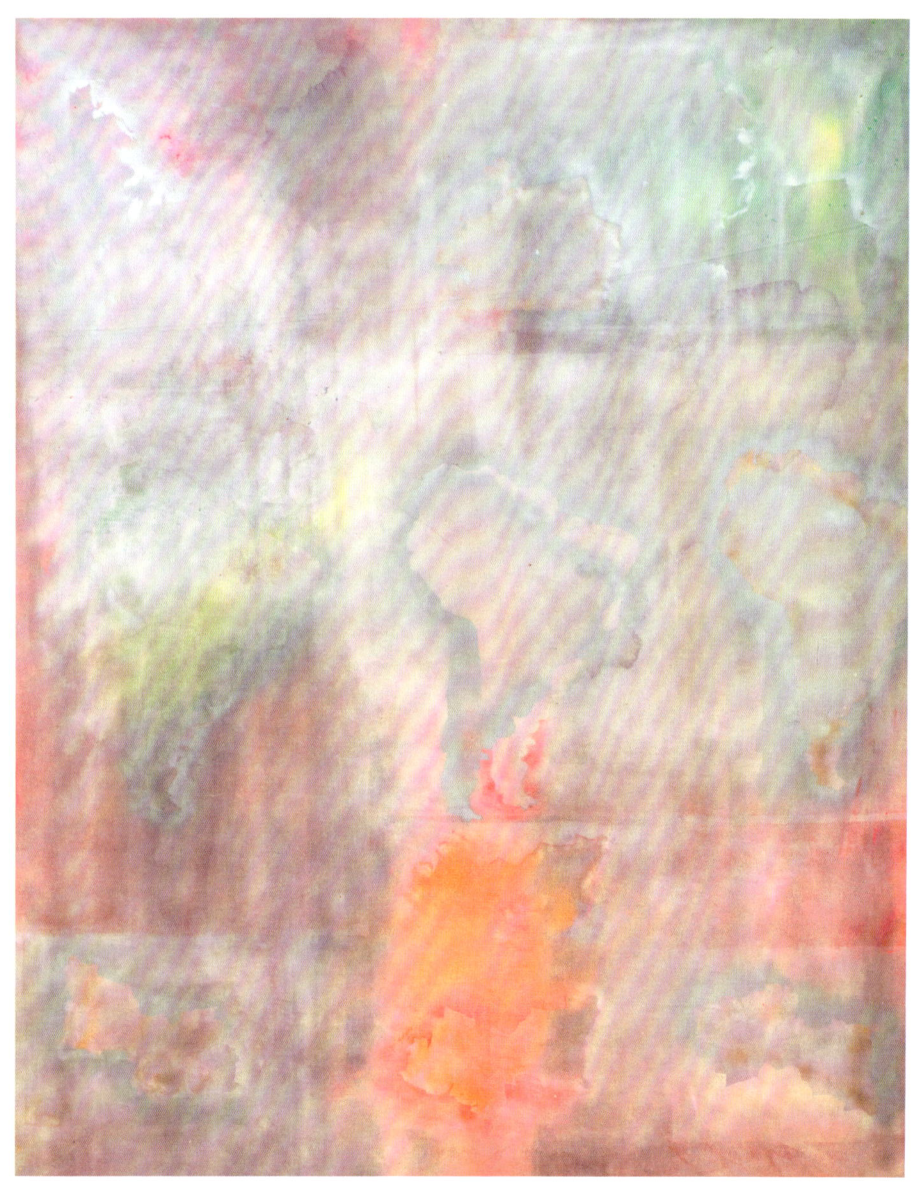

Raining Down South 1968
Acrylic paint and spray
paint on canvas
348.5 × 275.5

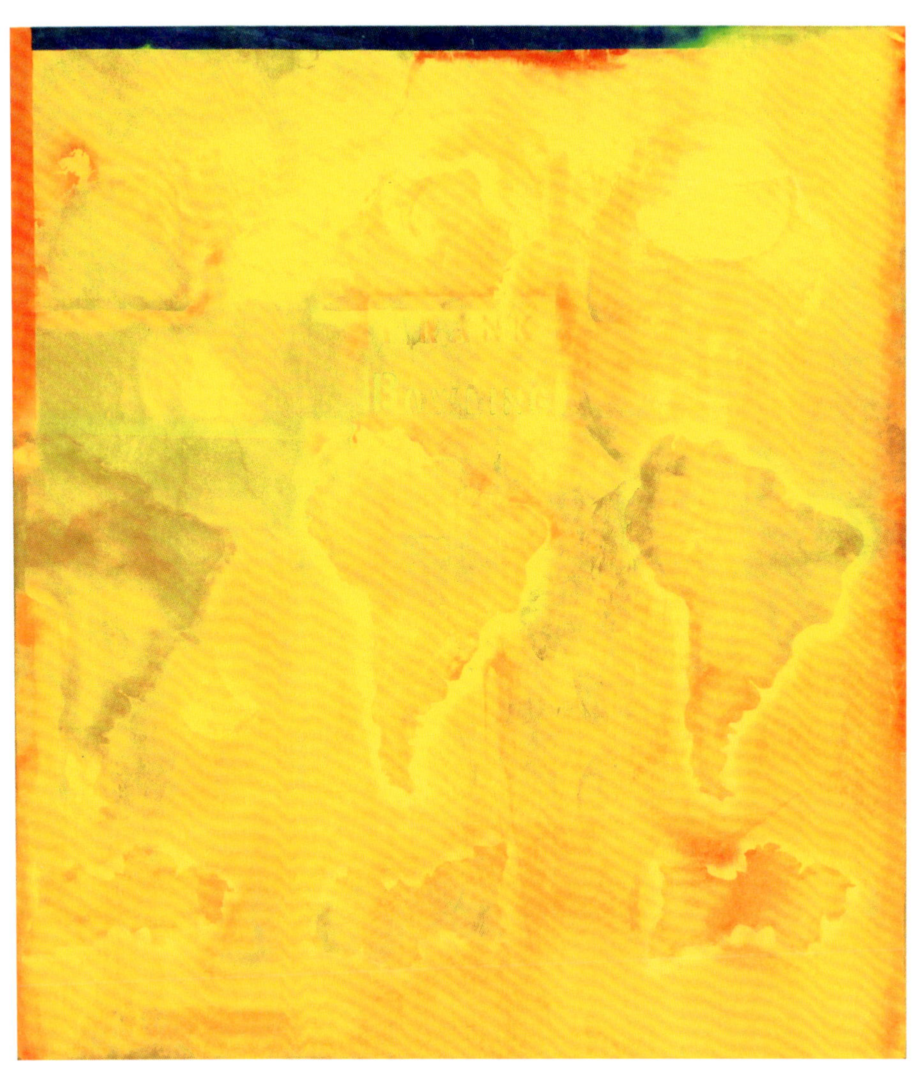

Mel Edwards Decides 1968
Acrylic paint and spray
paint on canvas
293 × 261

Schlesingerblue 1968
Acrylic paint and spray
paint on canvas
114 × 221

Night Journey 1969–70
Acrylic paint on canvas
213 × 182.9

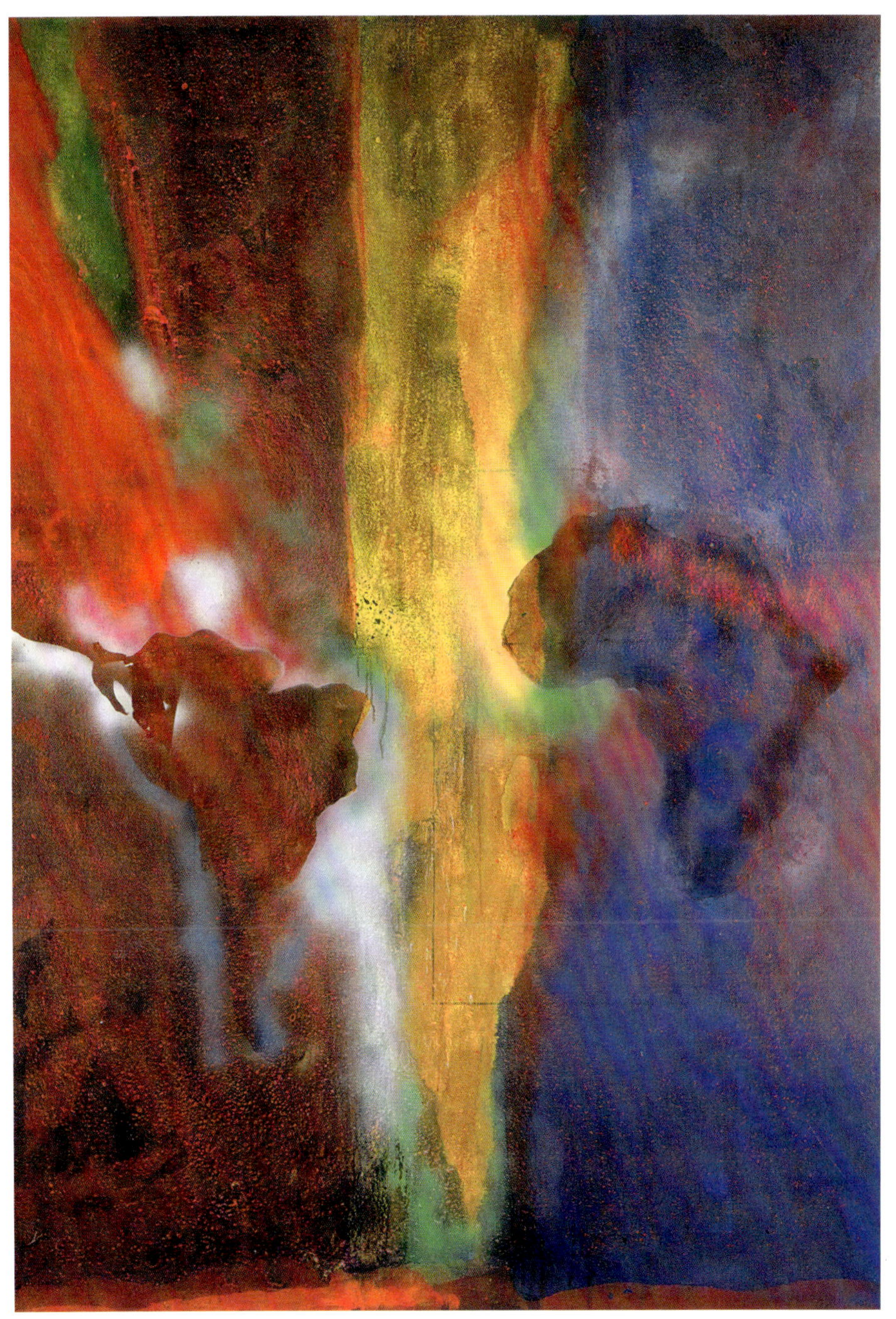

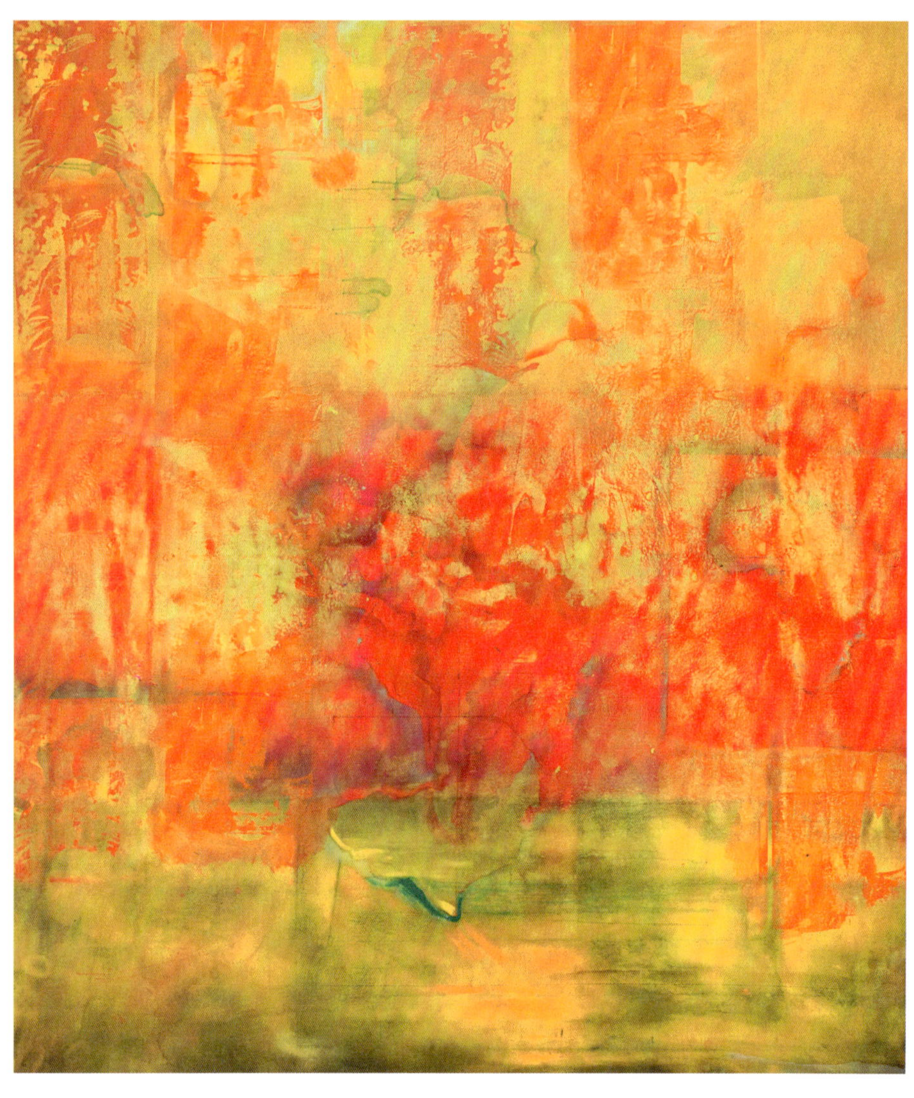

Middle Passage 1970
Acrylic paint and
silkscreened ink on canvas
321 × 281

Middle Passage 1970
Synthetic polymer paint,
silkscreened ink, spray
paint, wax crayon and
graphite on canvas
310.5 × 310.5

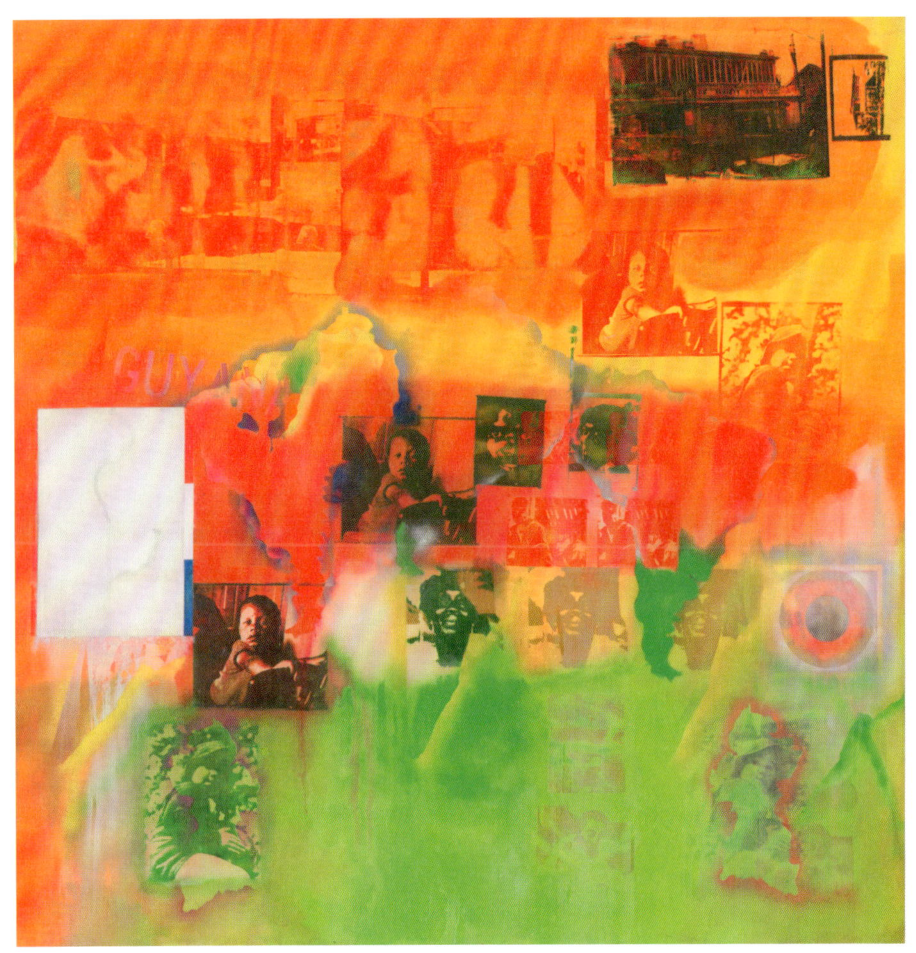

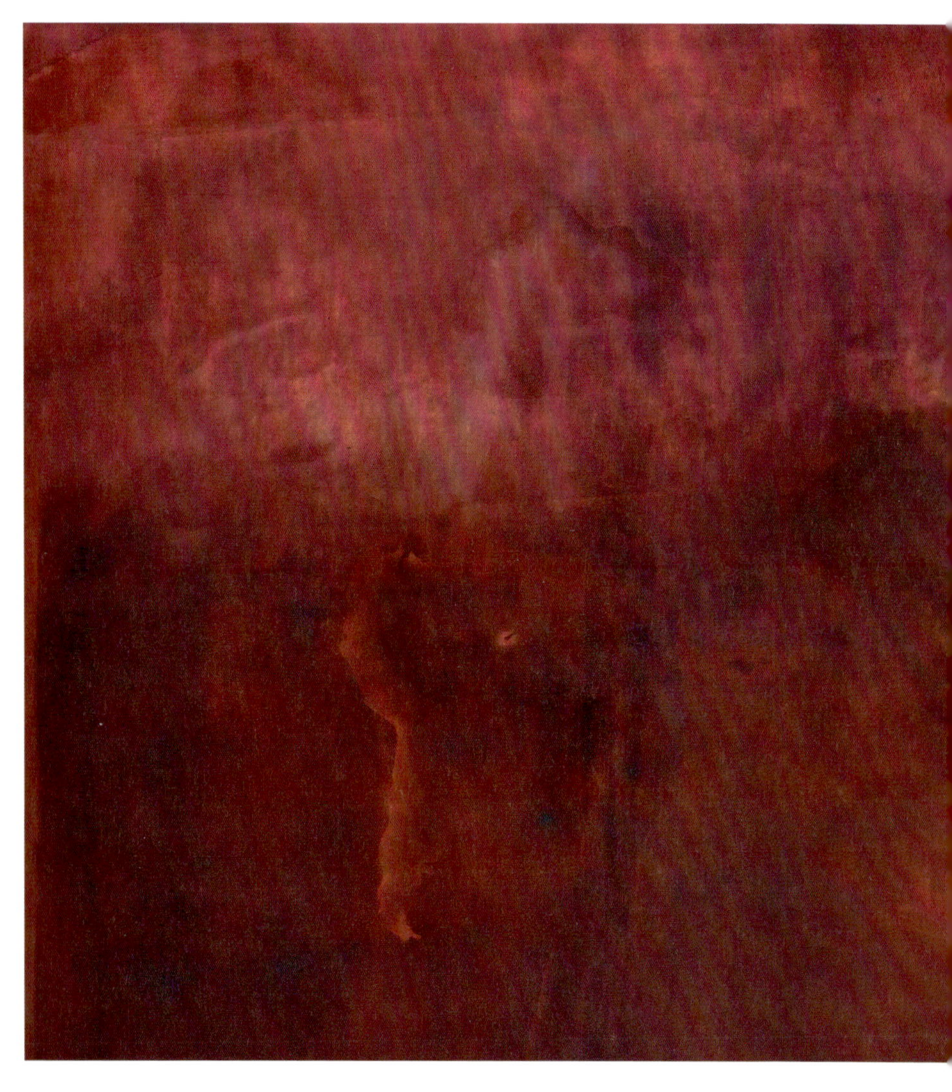

Marcia H. Travels 1970
Acrylic paint on canvas
282.5 × 541

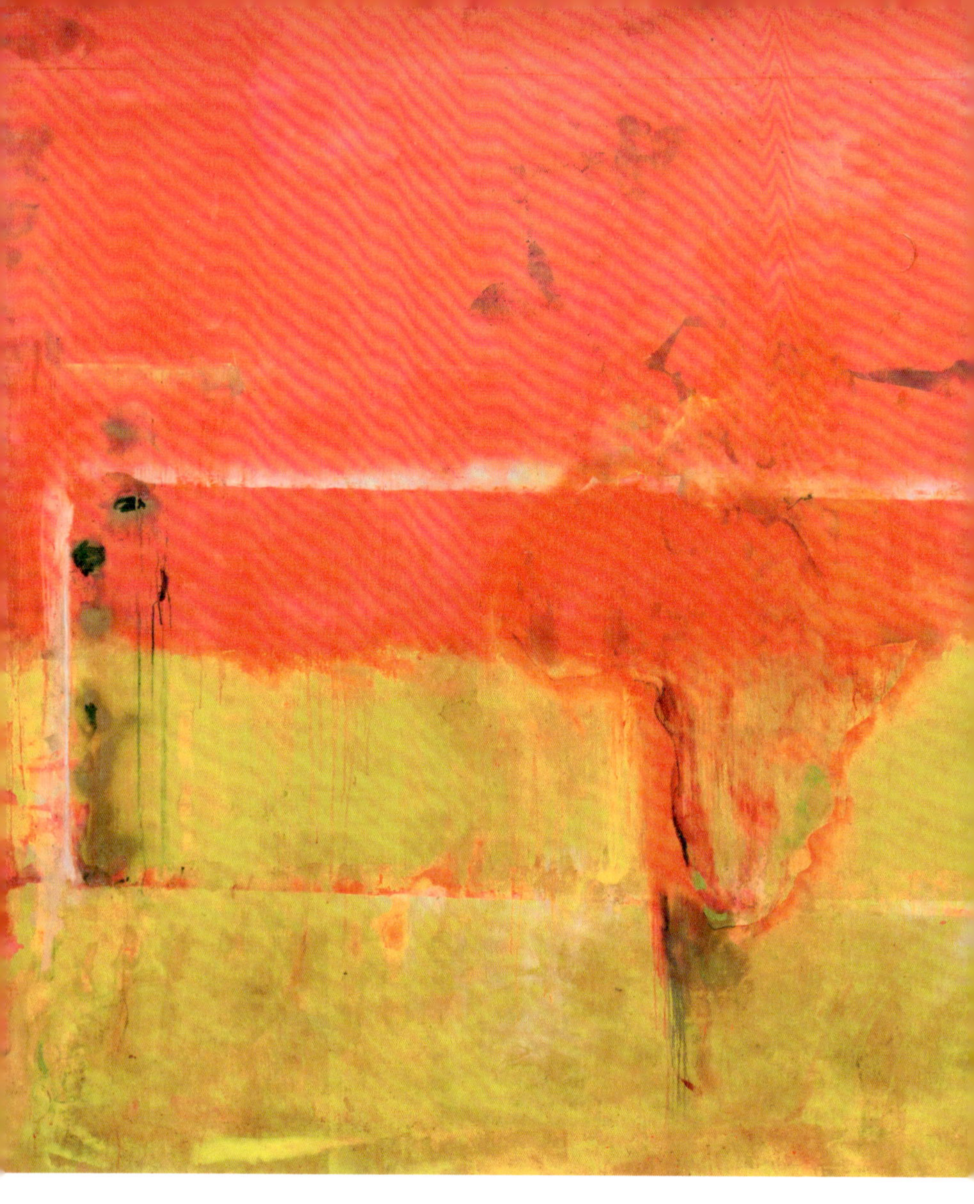

Dog Daze 1971
Acrylic paint and spray
paint on two canvases
273.6 × 492

Texas Louise 1971
Acrylic paint on canvas
282 × 665

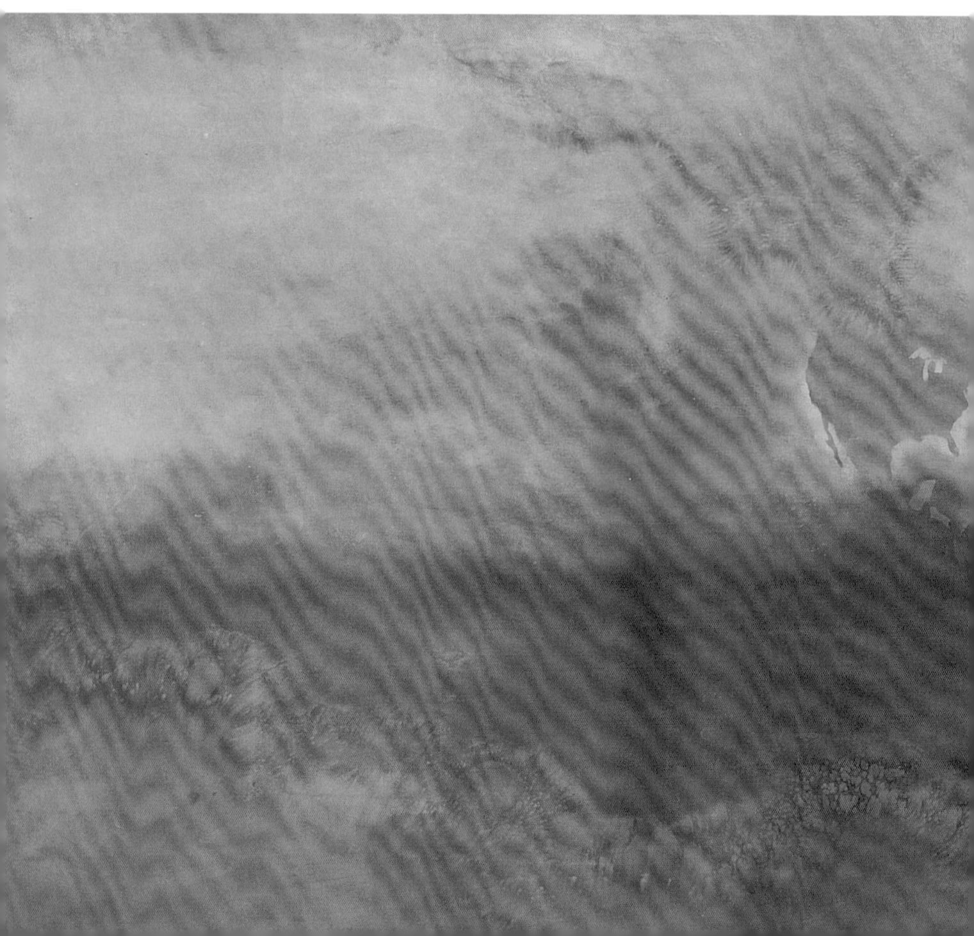

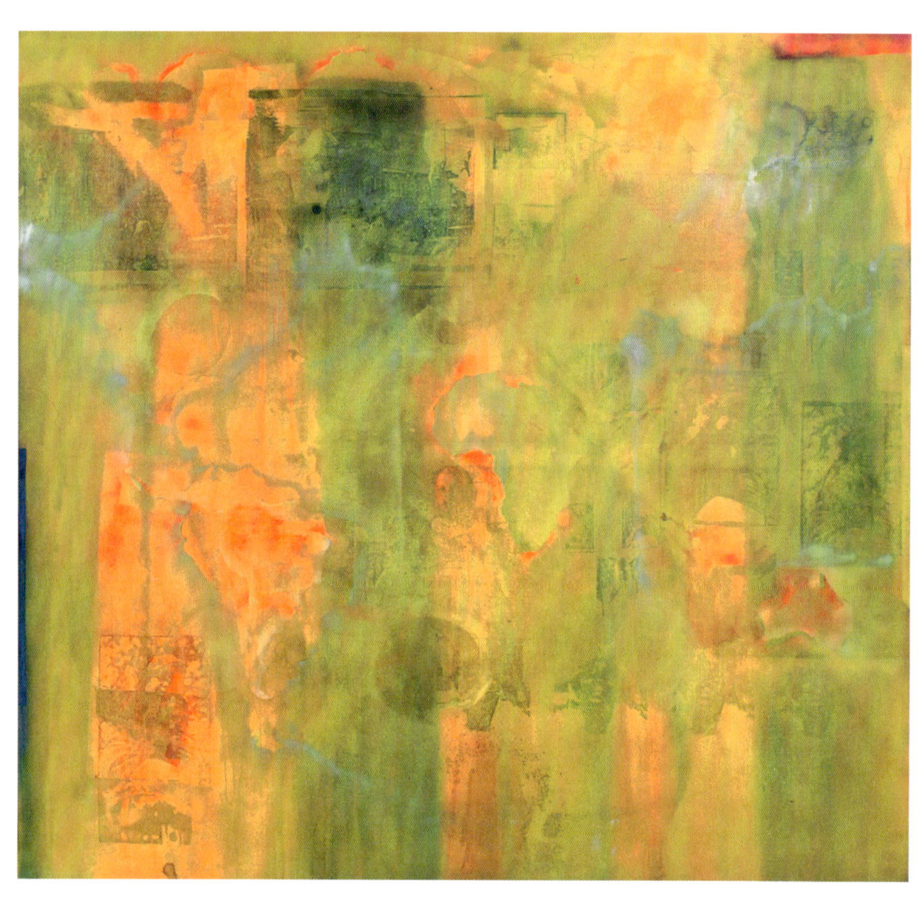

Where is Lucienne? 1971
Acrylic paint on canvas
308 × 337

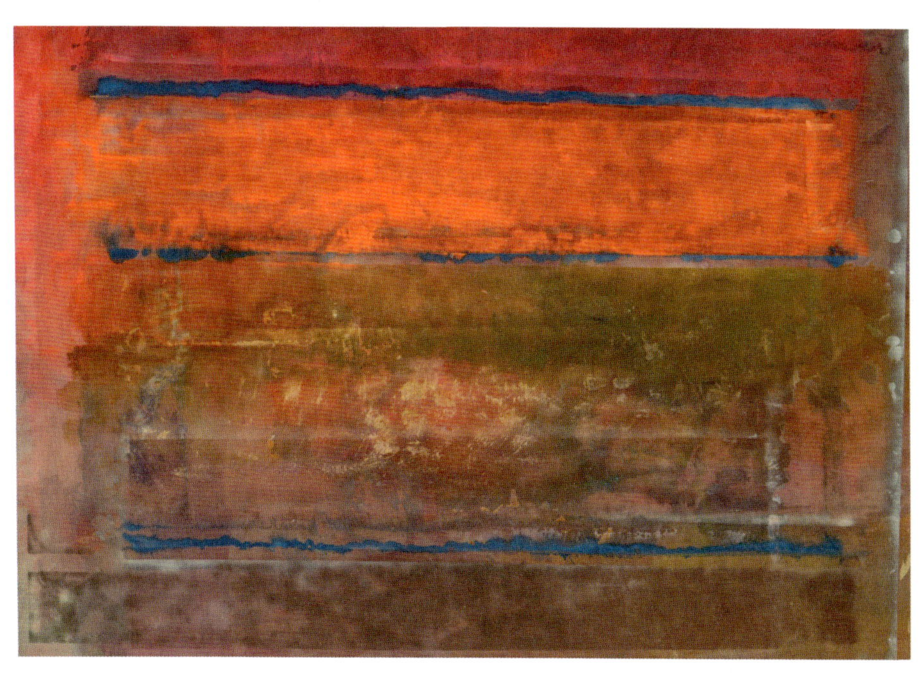

Rupununi 1971
Acrylic paint on canvas
284.8 × 415.4

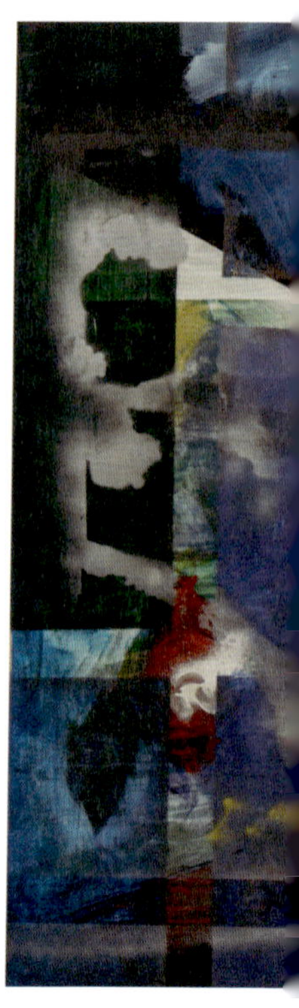

Polish Rebecca 1971
Acrylic paint and spray
paint on canvas
227 × 359

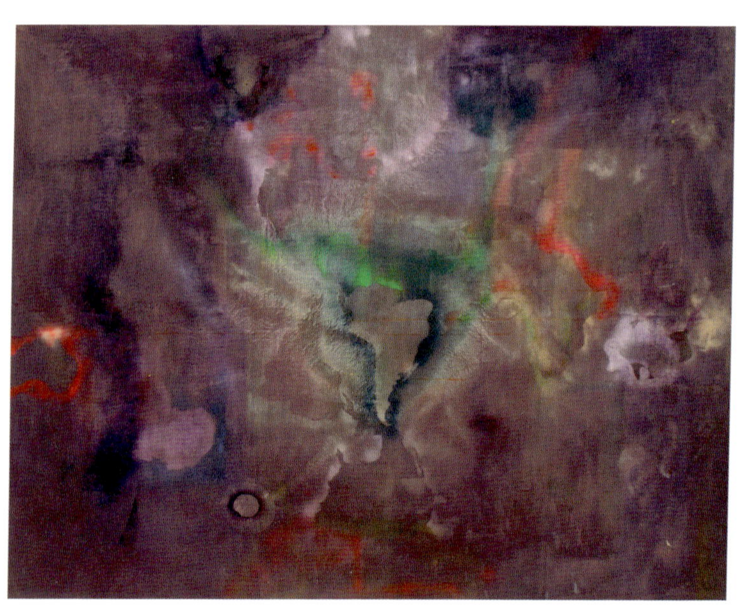

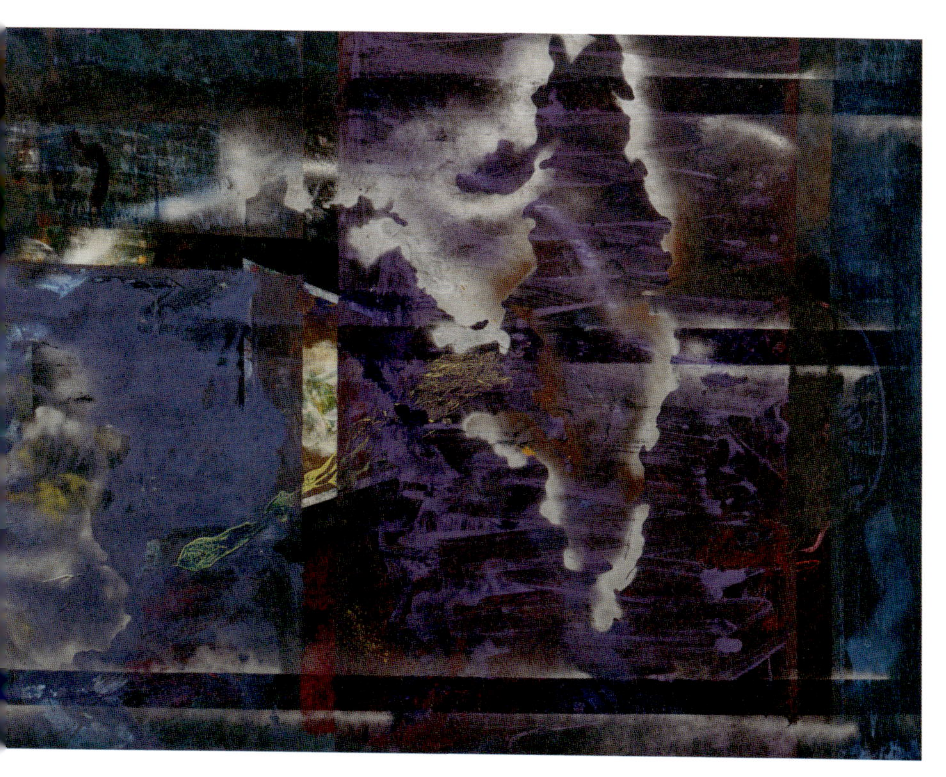

Upside Down 1971–2
Acrylic paint on canvas
159.4 × 274.3

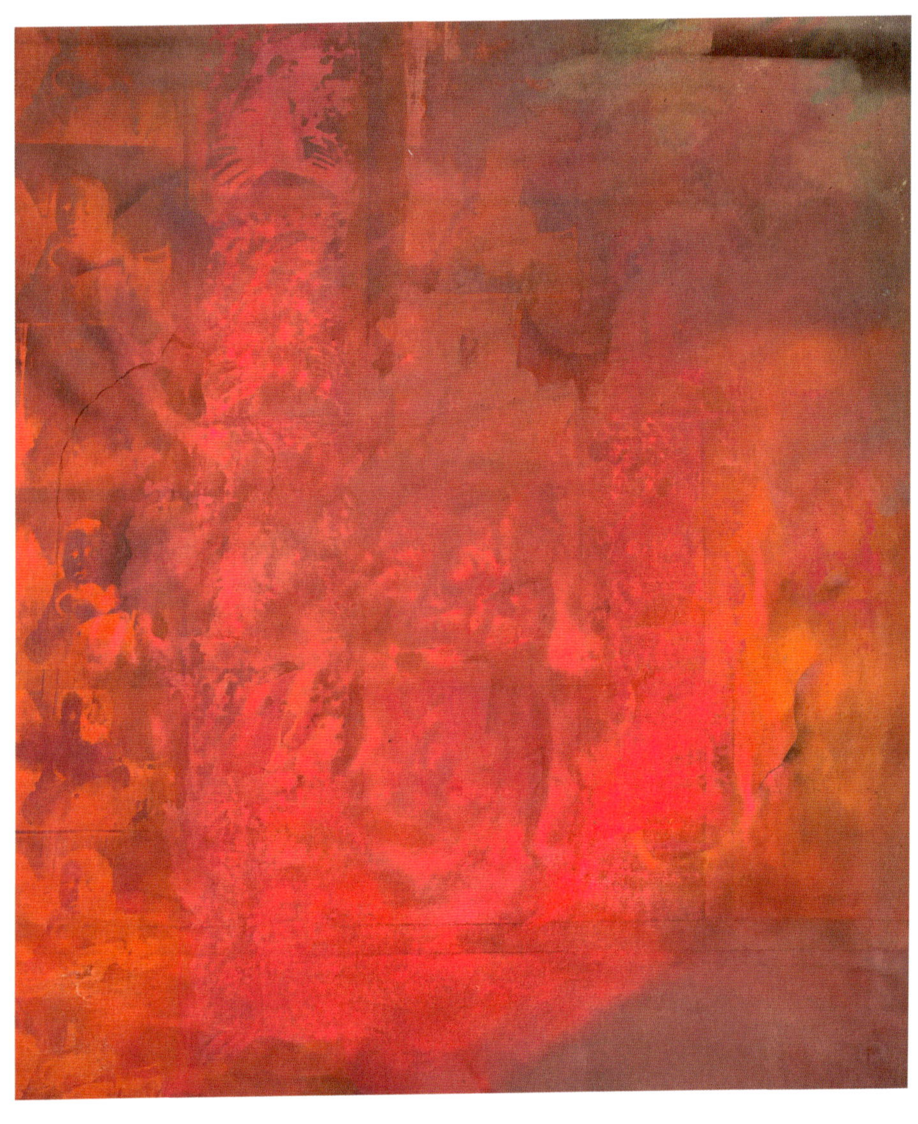

Dan & Them 1972
Acrylic paint on canvas
282 × 240

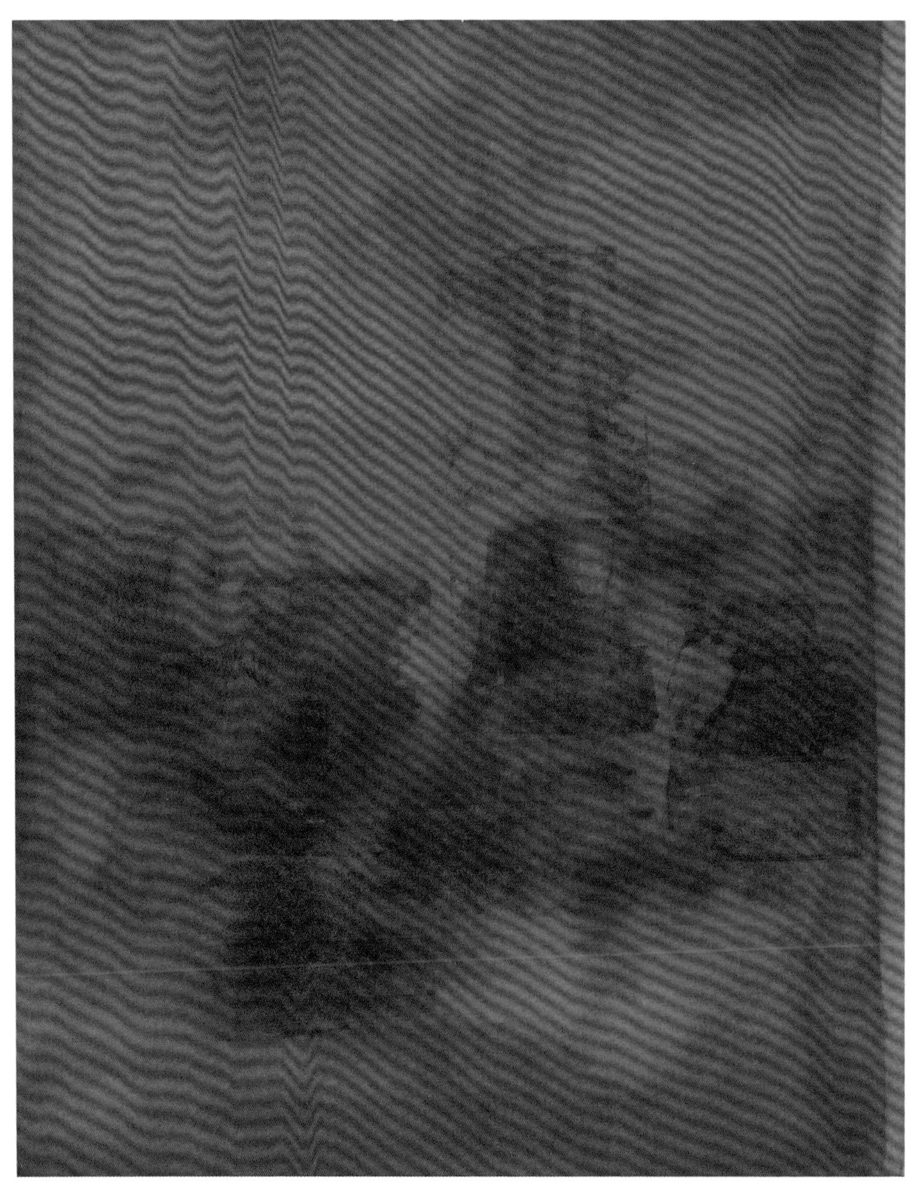

Doughlah G.E.P. 1968–70
Acrylic paint on canvas
228.6 × 182.6

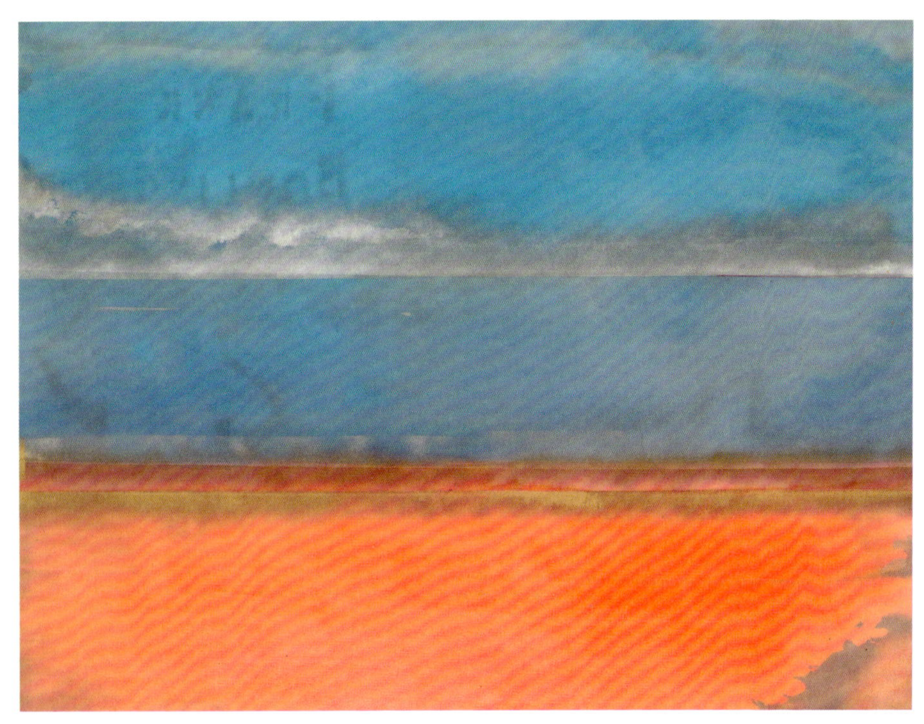

Looking at Barney and Mark
1972
Acrylic paint and spray
paint on canvas
167.5 × 228

Silver Fish ... for Susan 1972
Acrylic paint on canvas
160 × 228.6

For *Zephyr* 1973
Acrylic paint on canvas
170.5 × 170.5

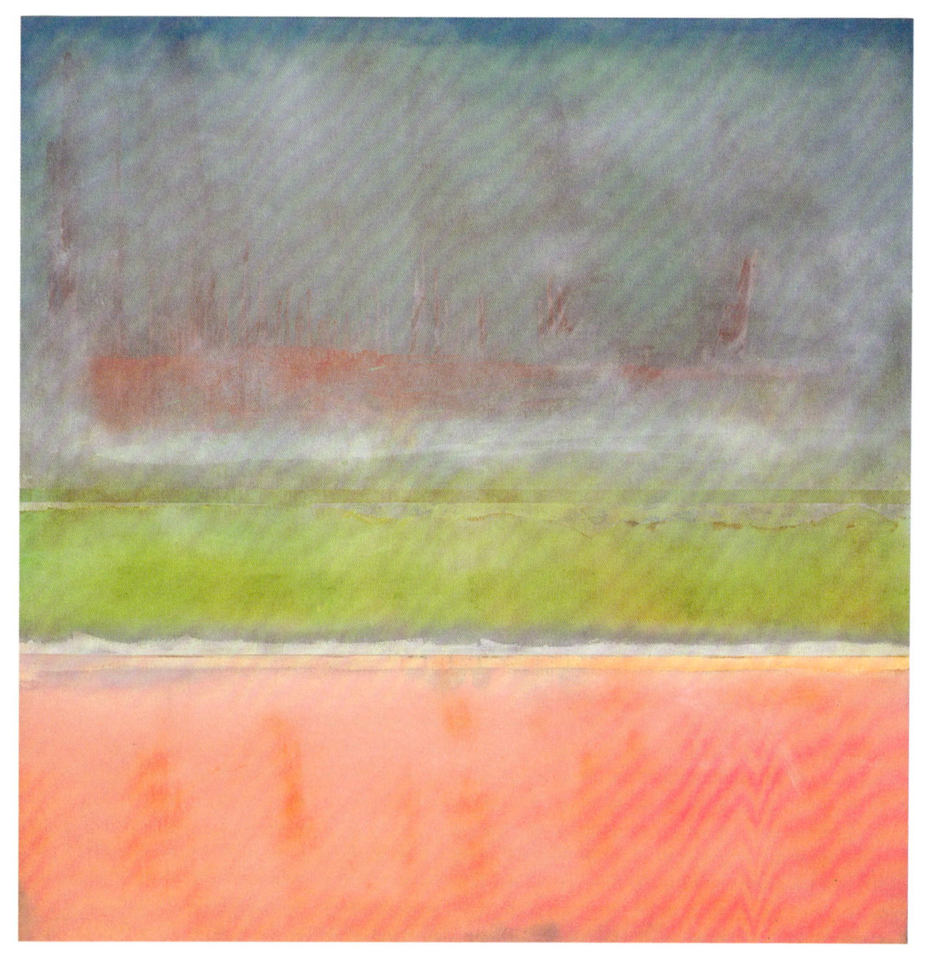

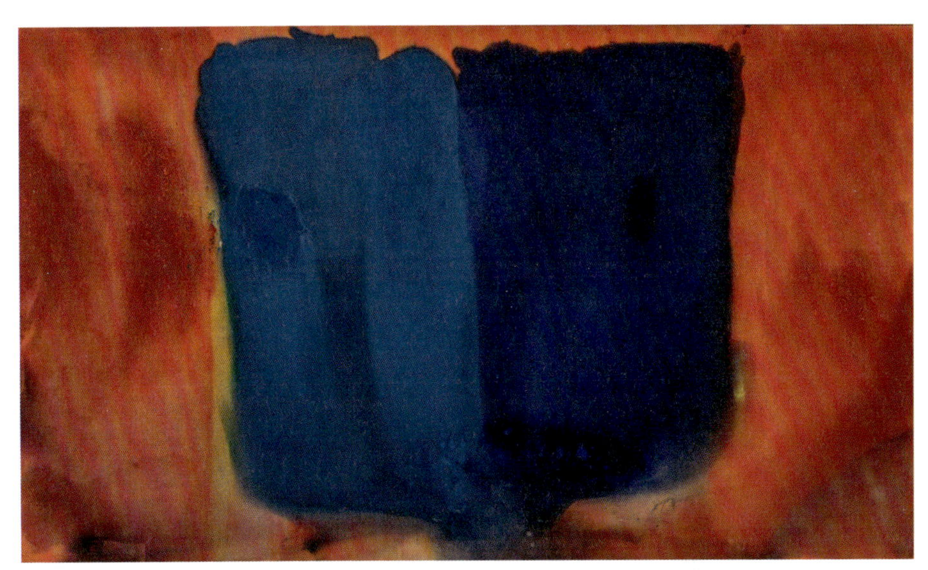

Two Blues, The Terminal Illness
1973
Acrylic paint on canvas
168.9 × 289.9

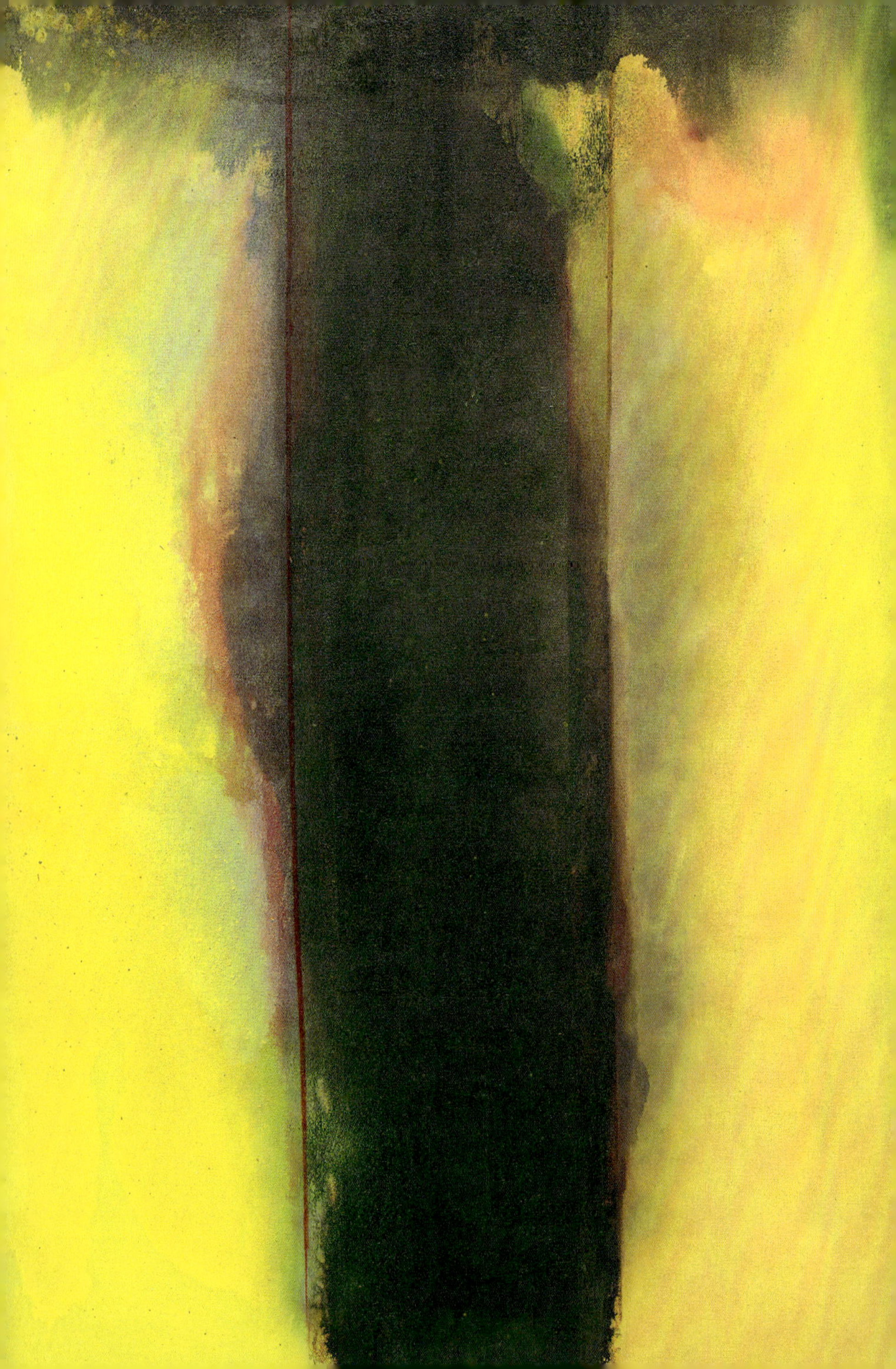

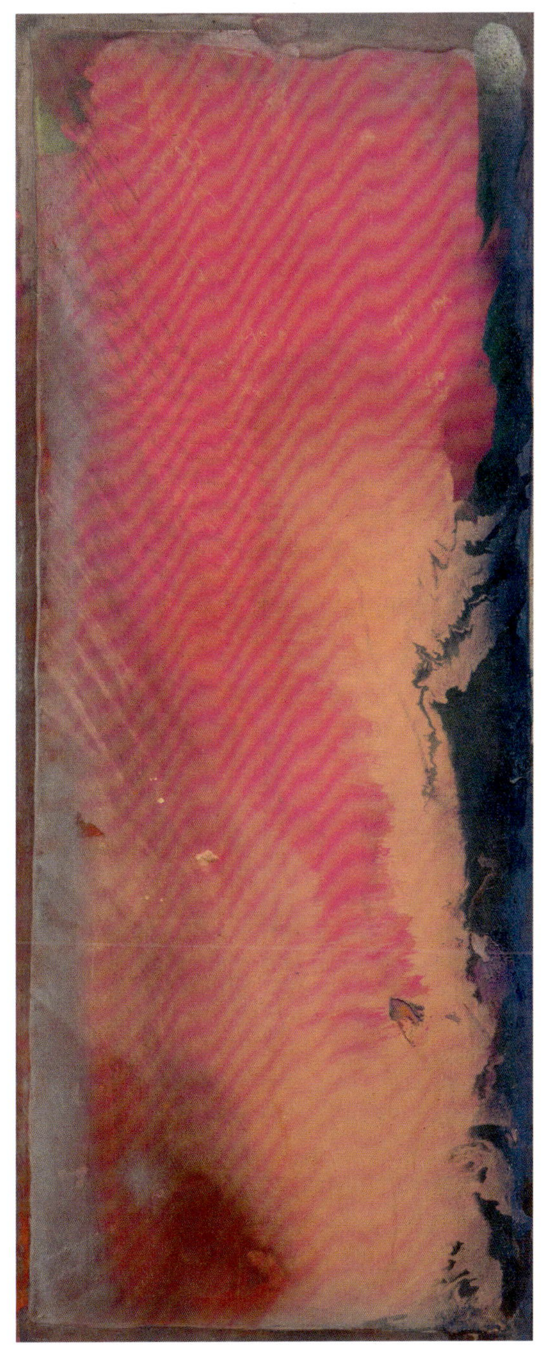

Giving Birth Astride a Grave
1973
Acrylic paint and vinyl
paint on canvas
183.5 × 122.7

Corinna's Adam 1974
Acrylic paint on canvas
200.5 × 84

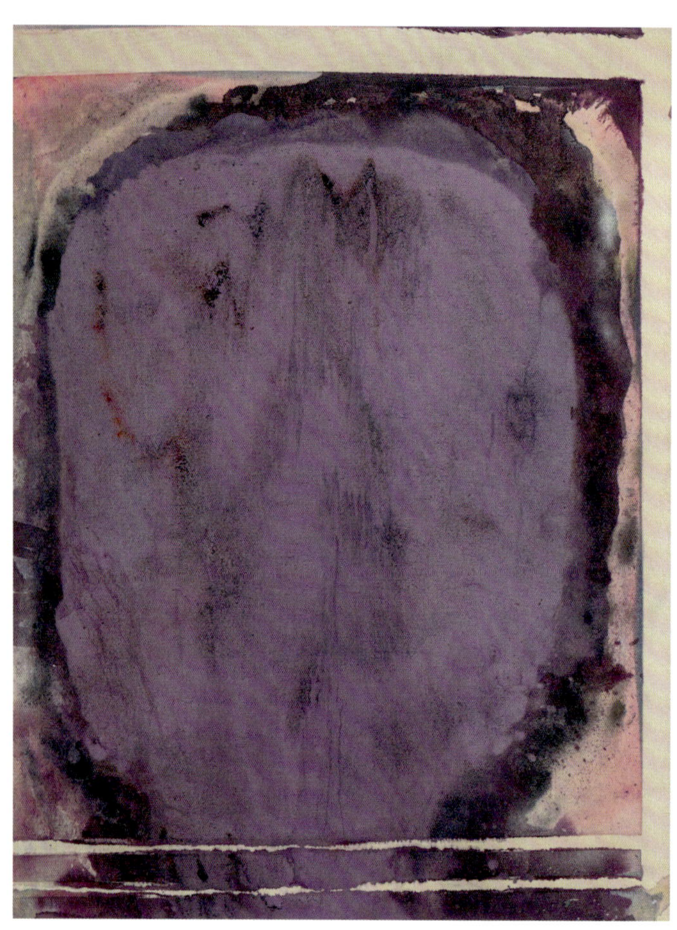

Head 1974
Acrylic paint on canvas
147.3 × 111.8

Ziff 1974
Acrylic paint on canvas
201 × 146

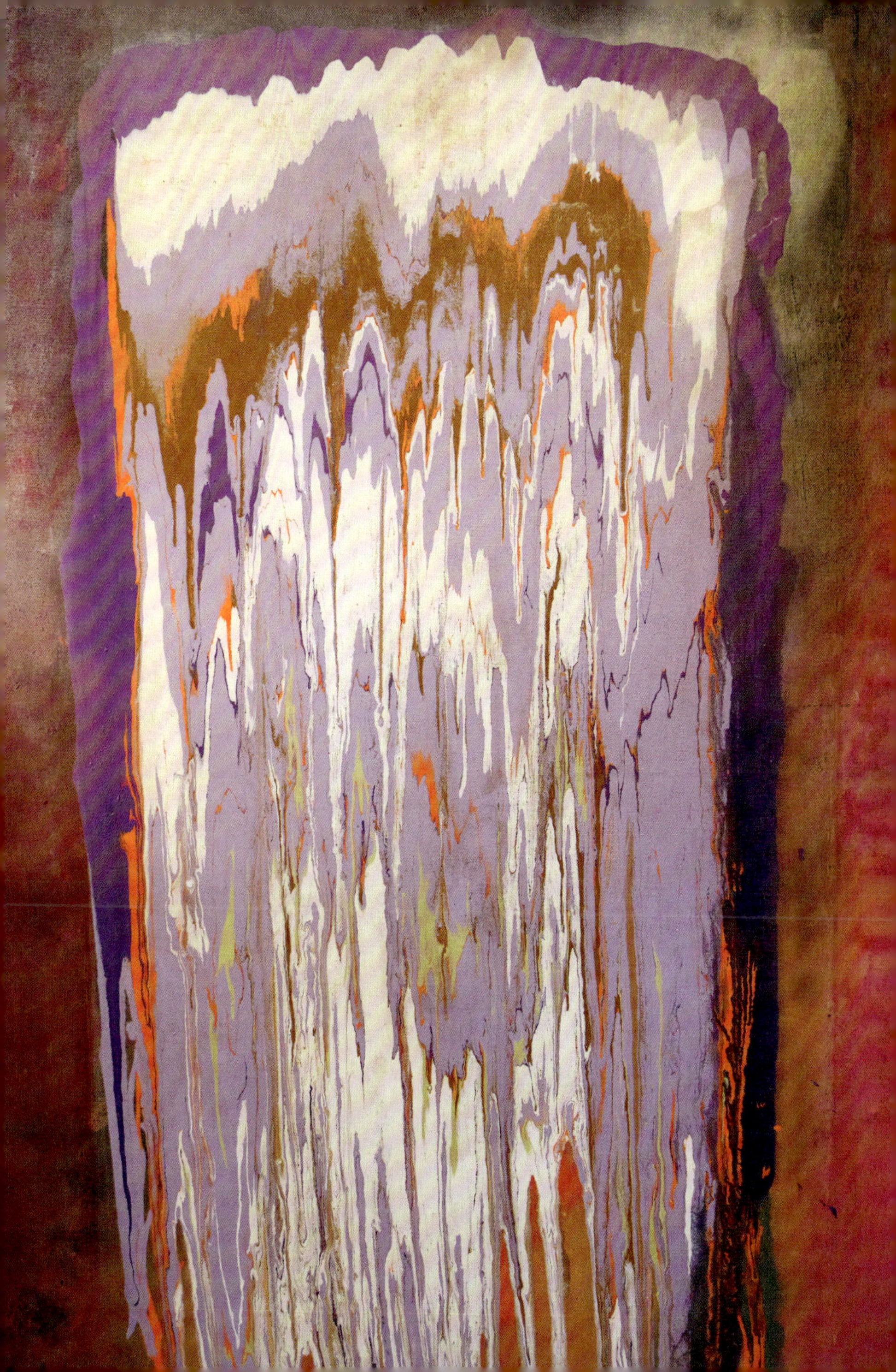

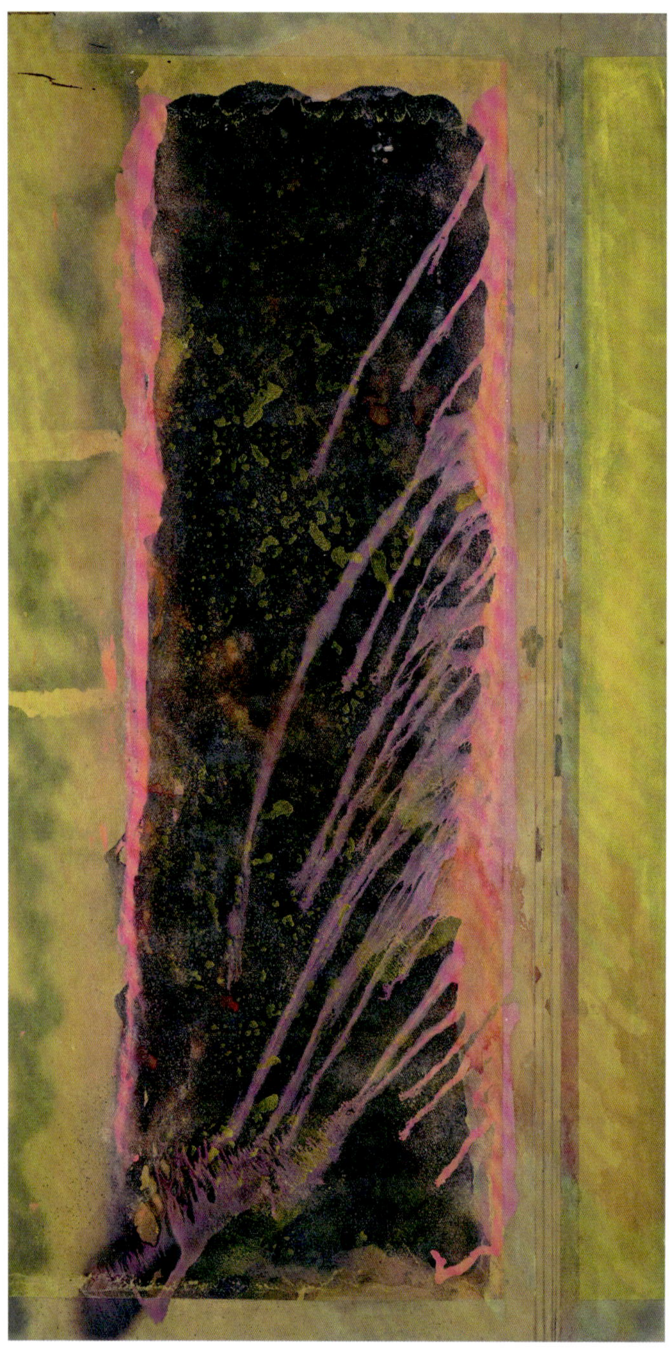

Trampoline 1975
Acrylic paint on canvas
223.5 × 111.8

Simon and Matthew 1975
Acrylic paint on canvas
228.5 × 119.5

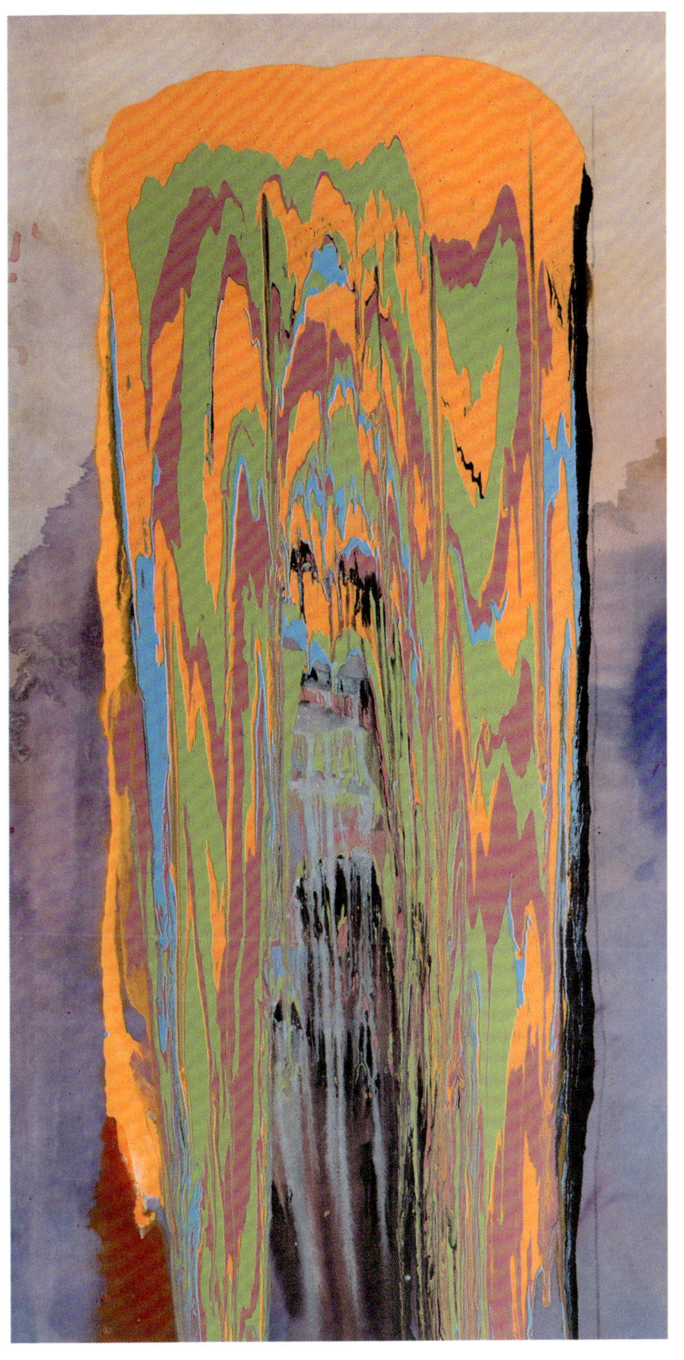

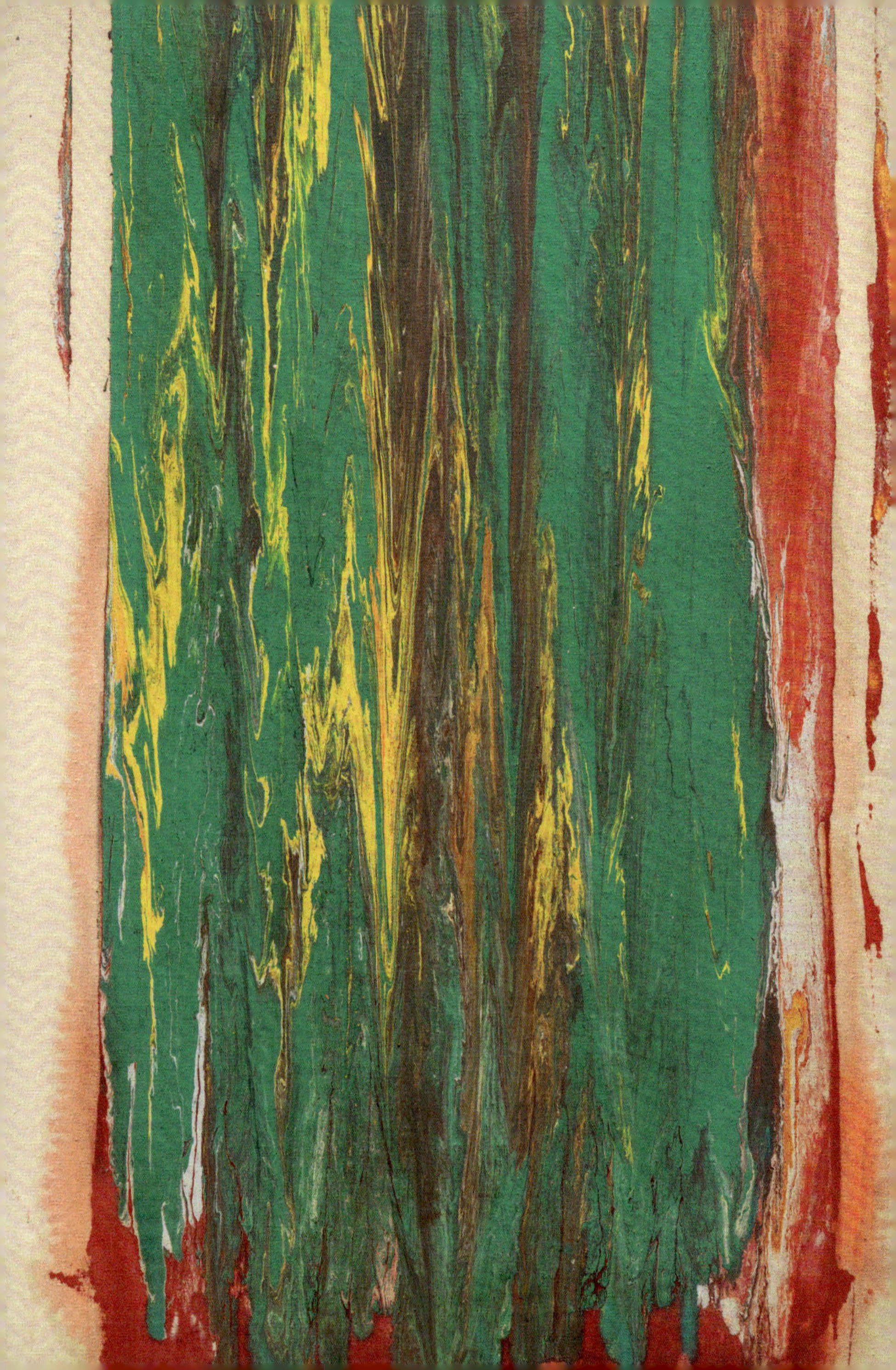

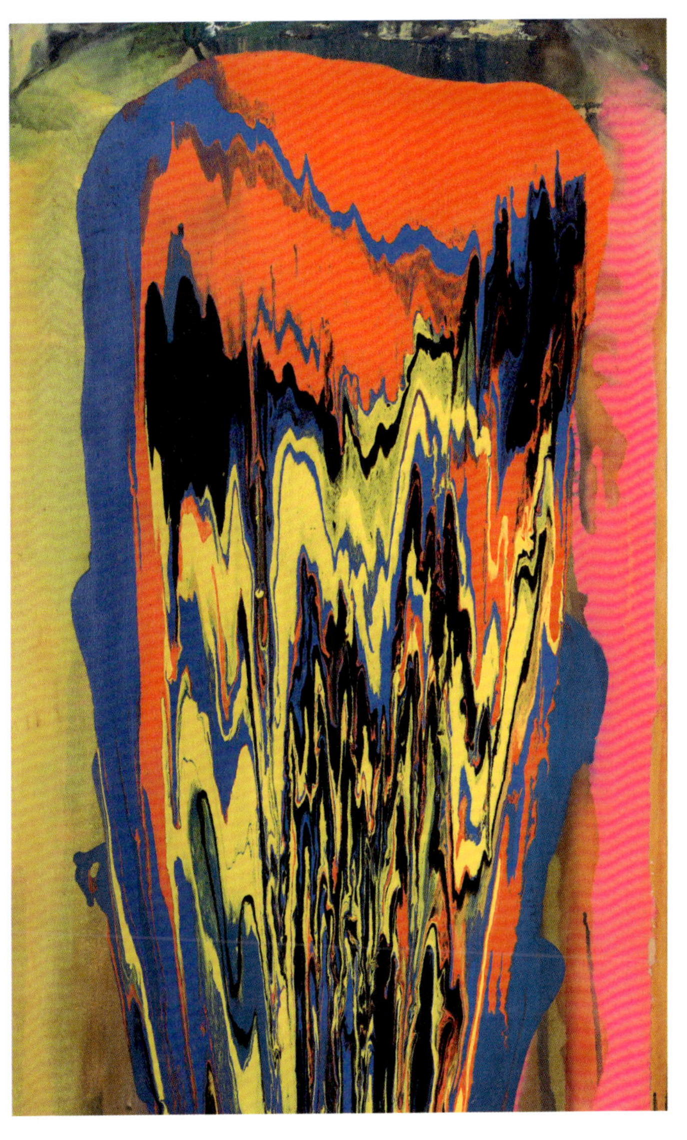

Jean Askew (the Weaver)
at Home 1971
Acrylic paint on canvas
90.5 × 60.5

Tony's Anvil 1975
Acrylic paint on canvas
173 × 107

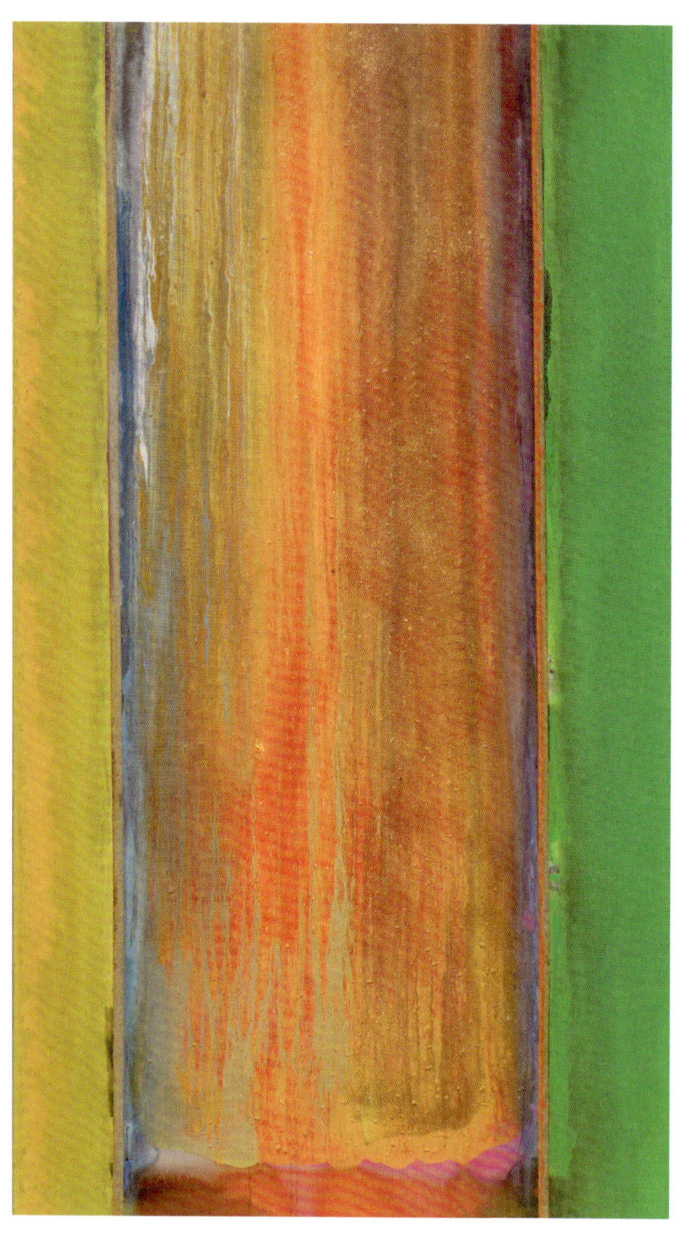

Suncrush 1976
Acrylic paint on canvas
208 × 116

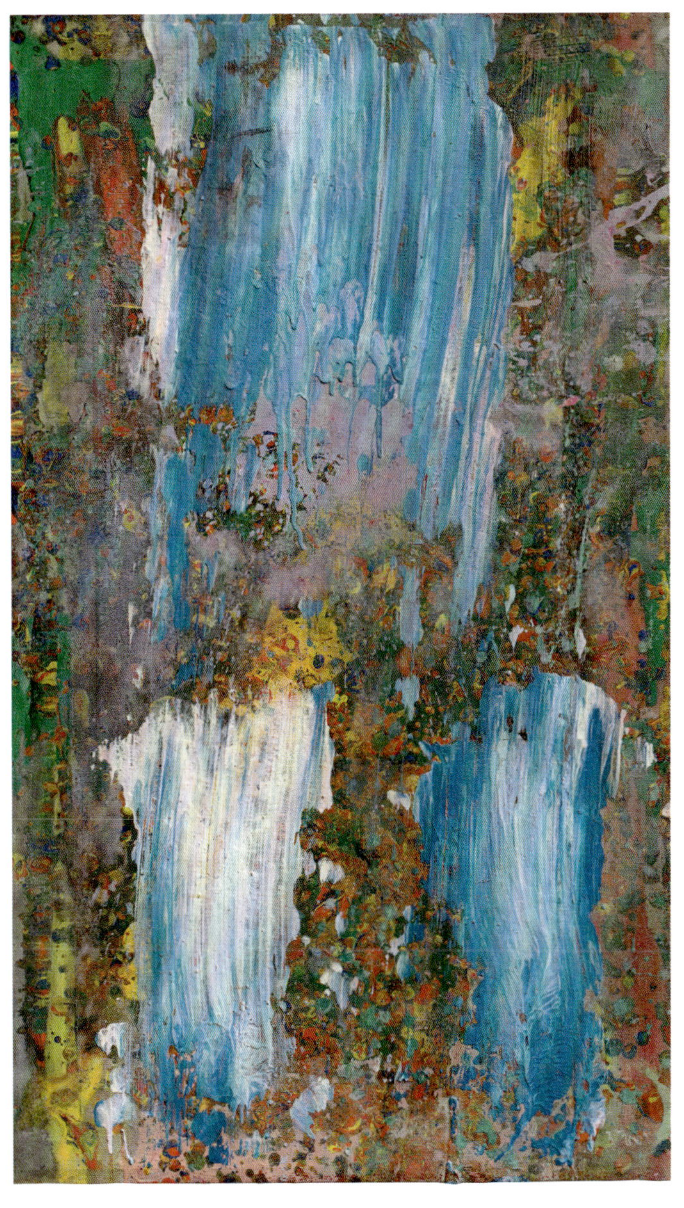

At Swim Two Manatee 1977–8
Acrylic paint on canvas
116.4 × 68.5

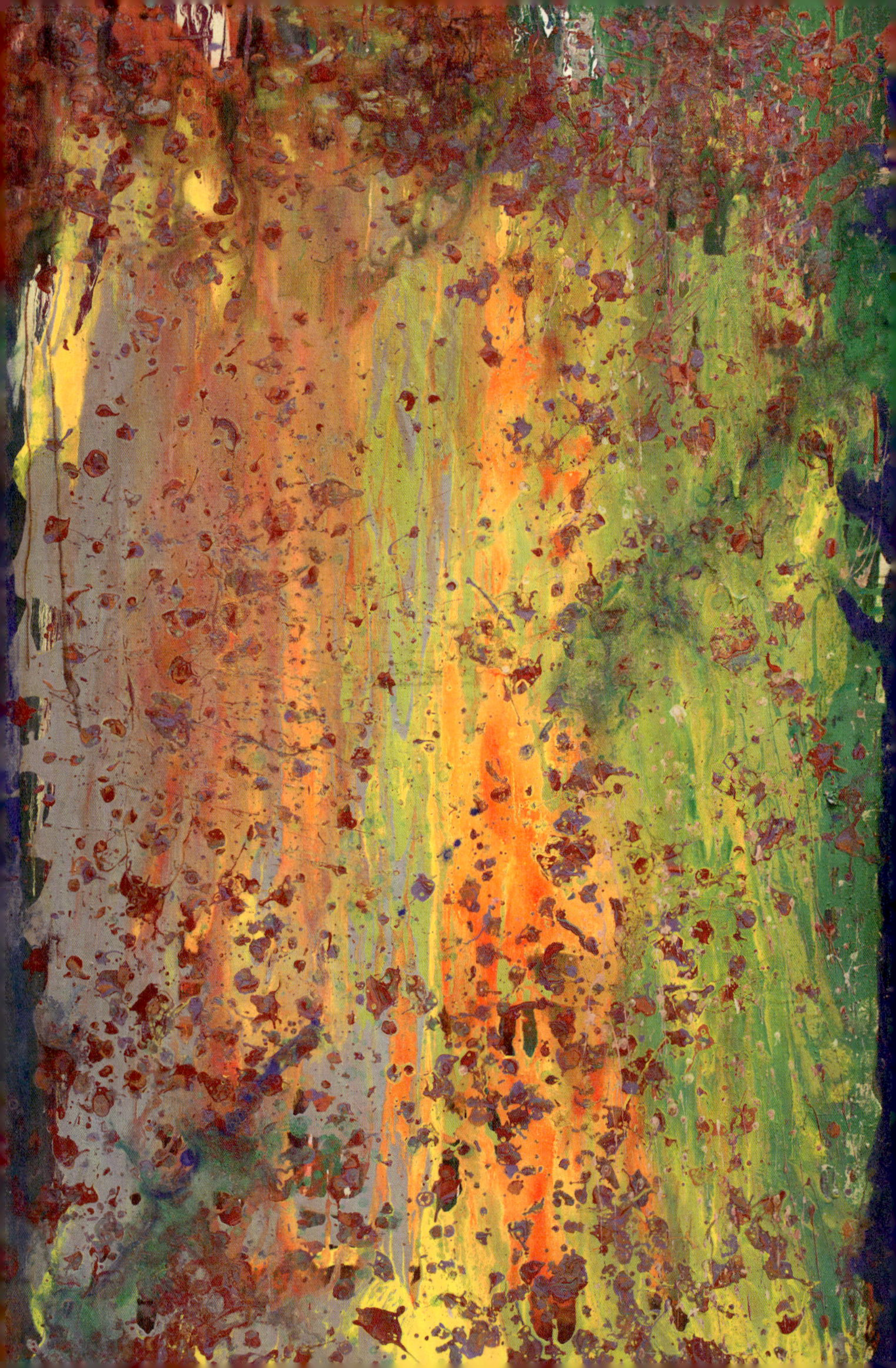

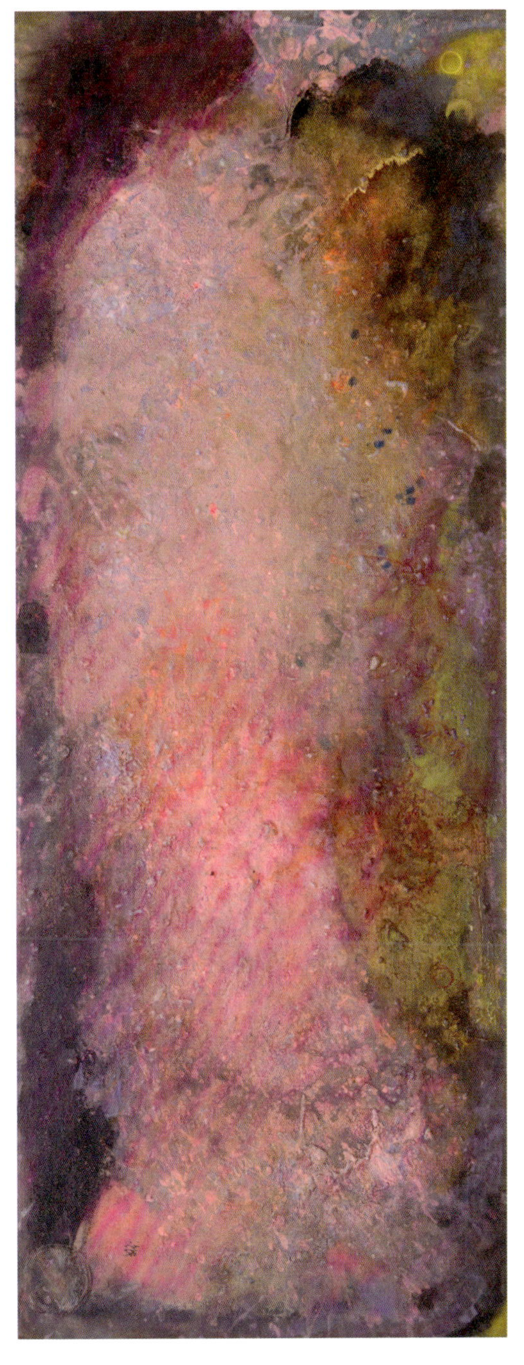

Jack 1978
Acrylic paint on canvas
203 × 130

Devil's Sole 1980
Acrylic paint on canvas
183 × 72

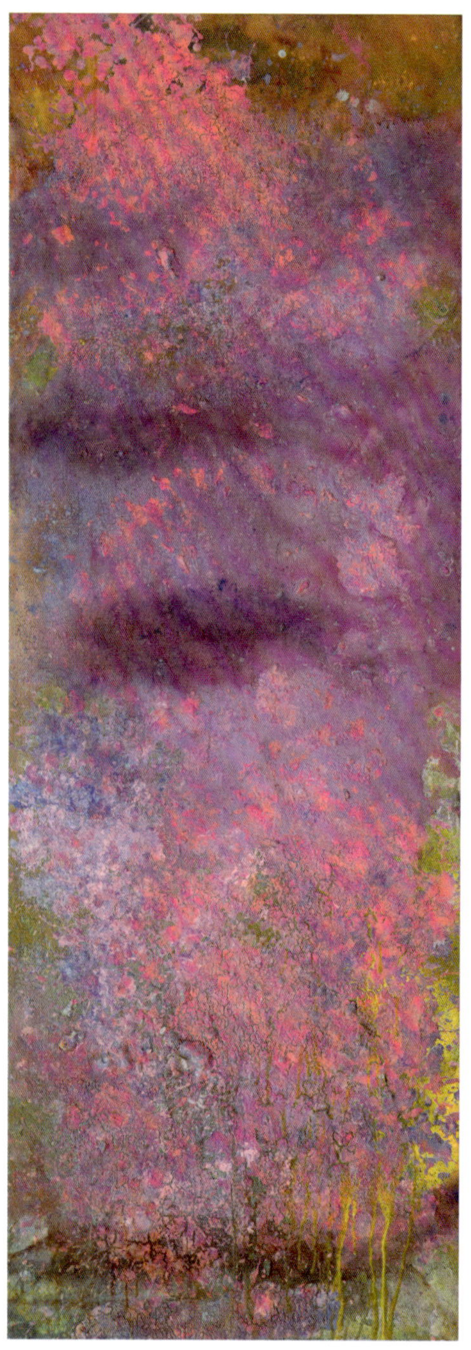

Mazarunitankfeat 1979
Acrylic paint on canvas
178 × 64

Moby Dick 1981
Acrylic paint on canvas
250.5 × 189

OVERLEAF
Serpentine 1982
Acrylic paint, acrylic gel,
acrylic foam and other
materials on canvas
171 × 274

Towards Crab Island 1983
Acrylic paint, acrylic gel,
acrylic foam and other
materials on canvas
175.3 × 289.6

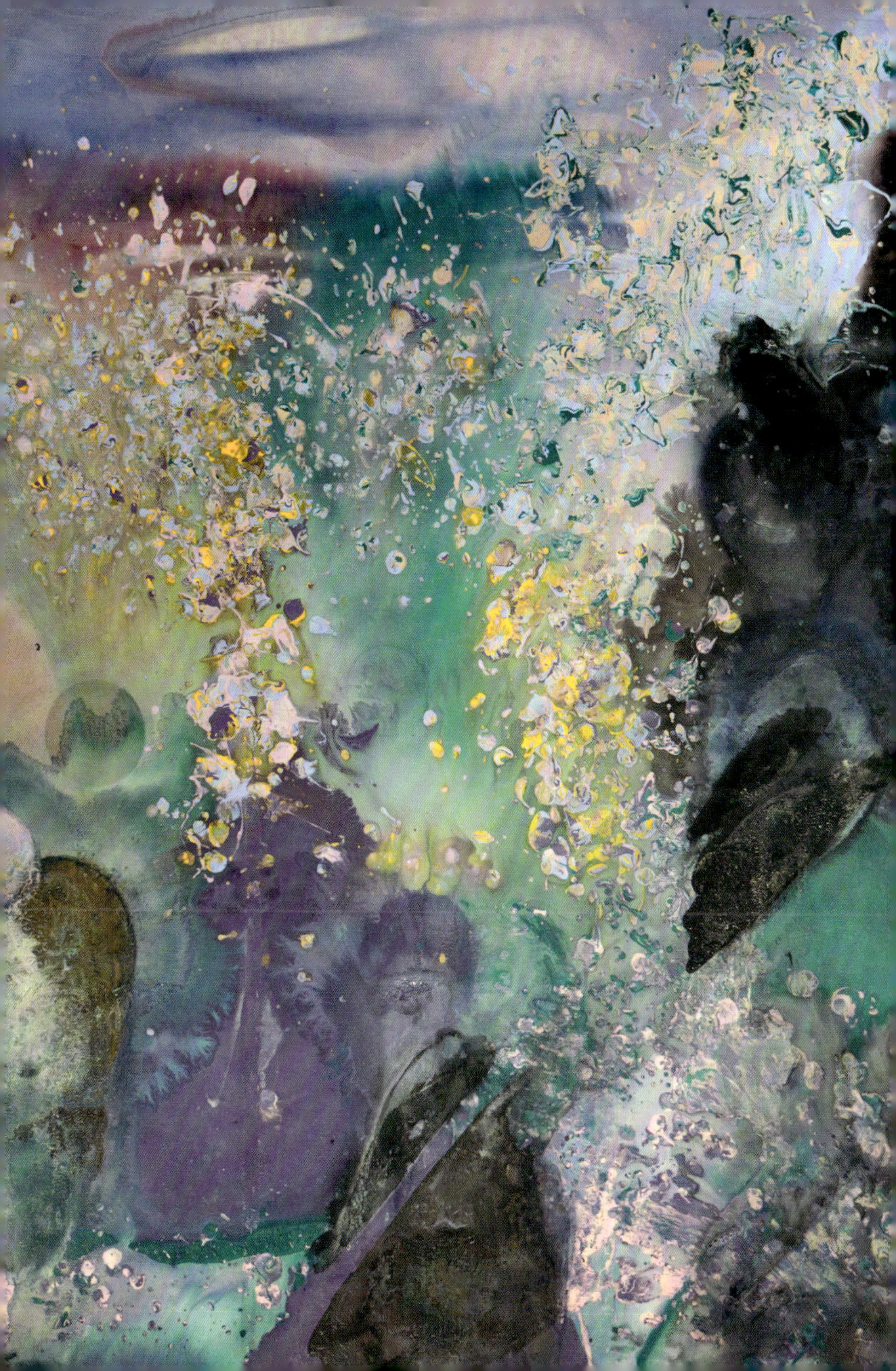

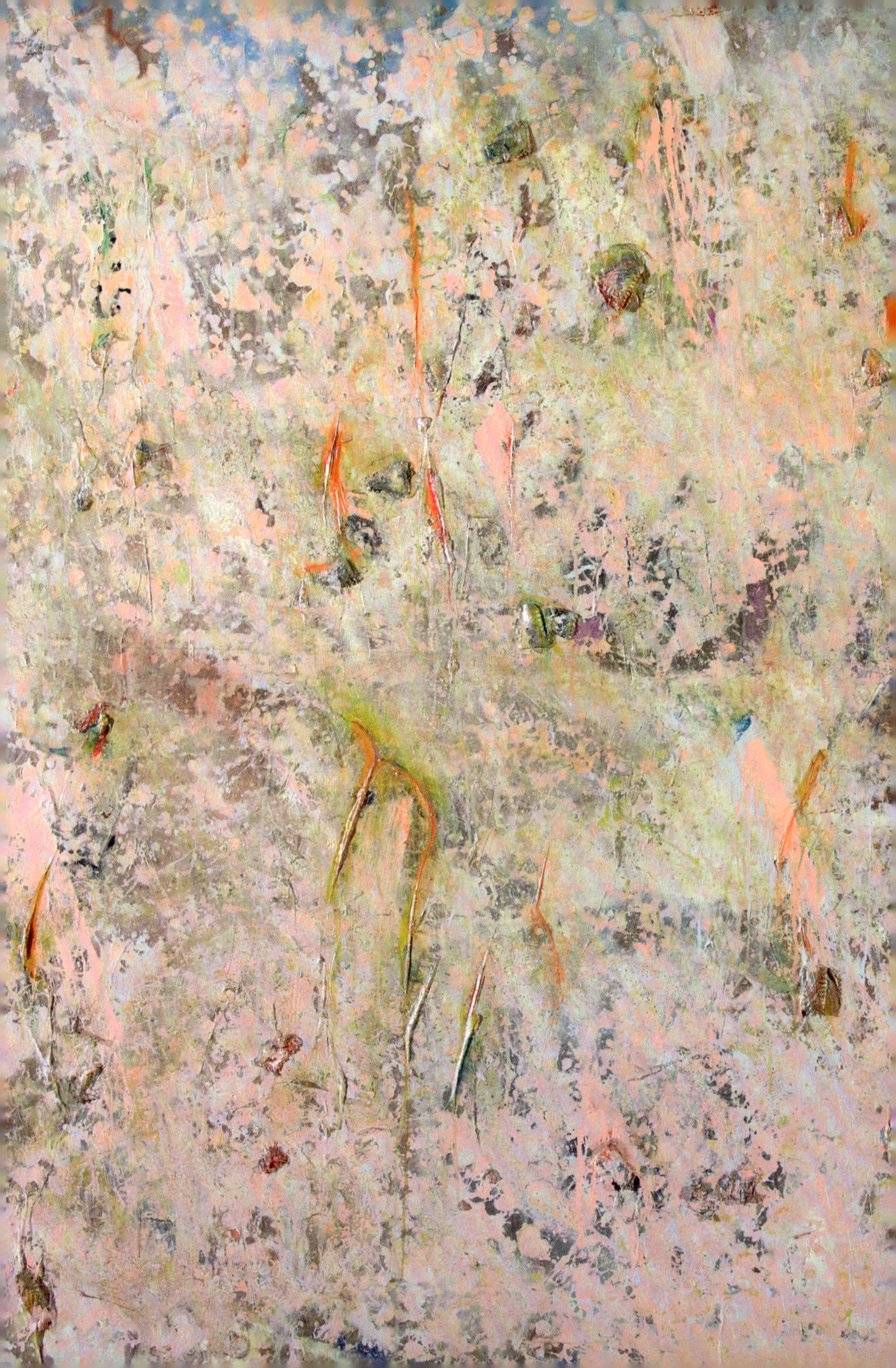

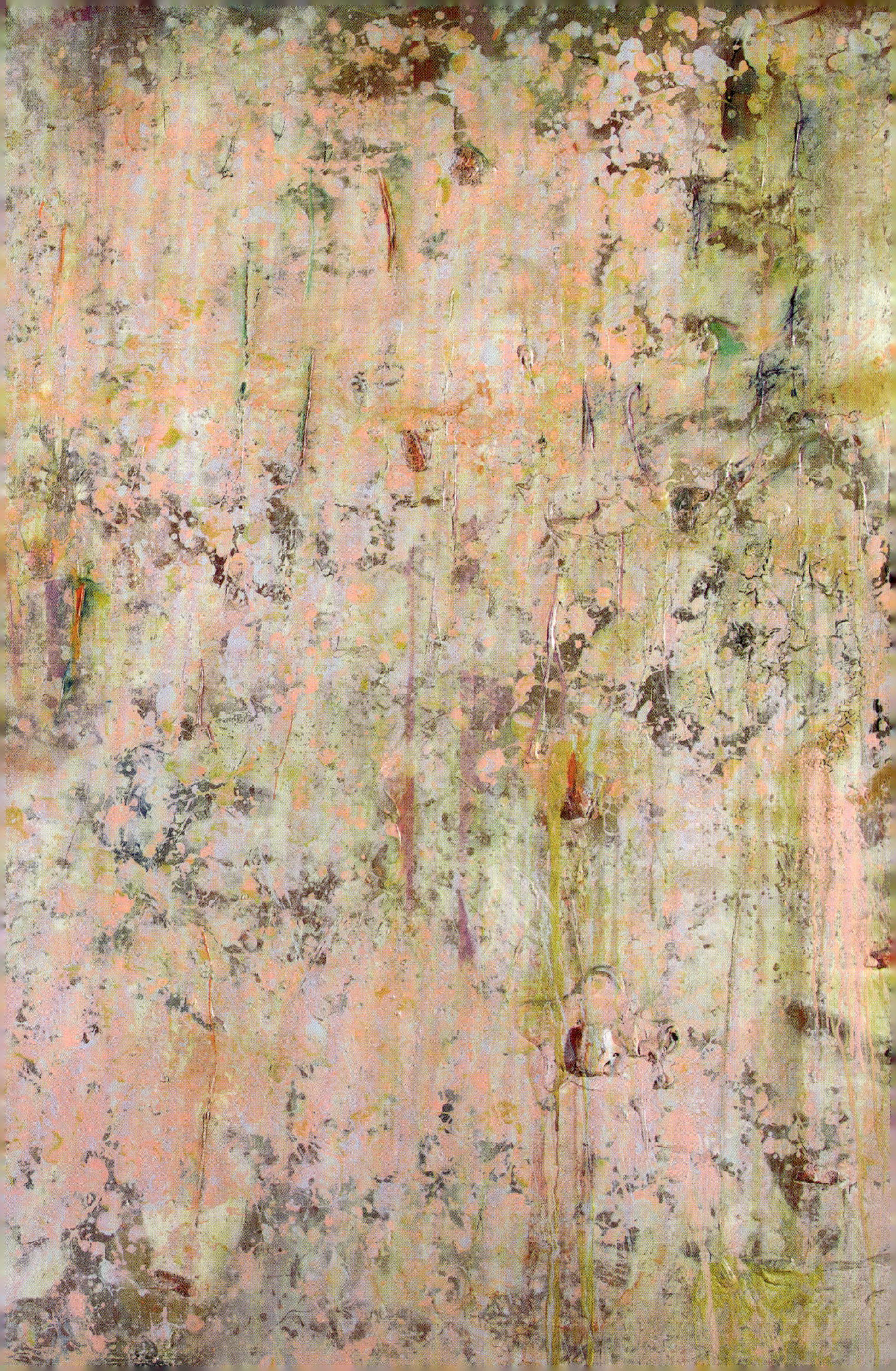

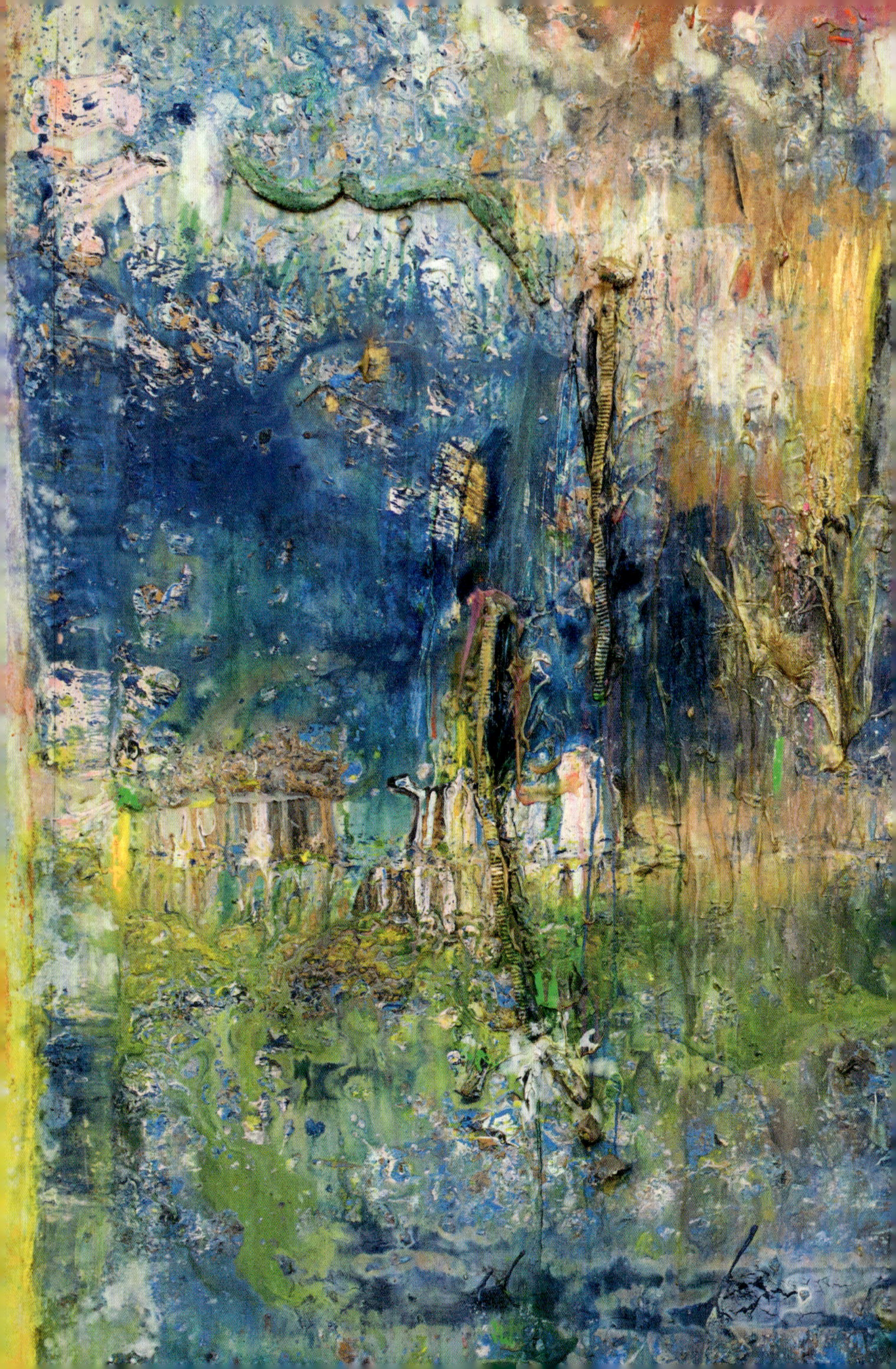

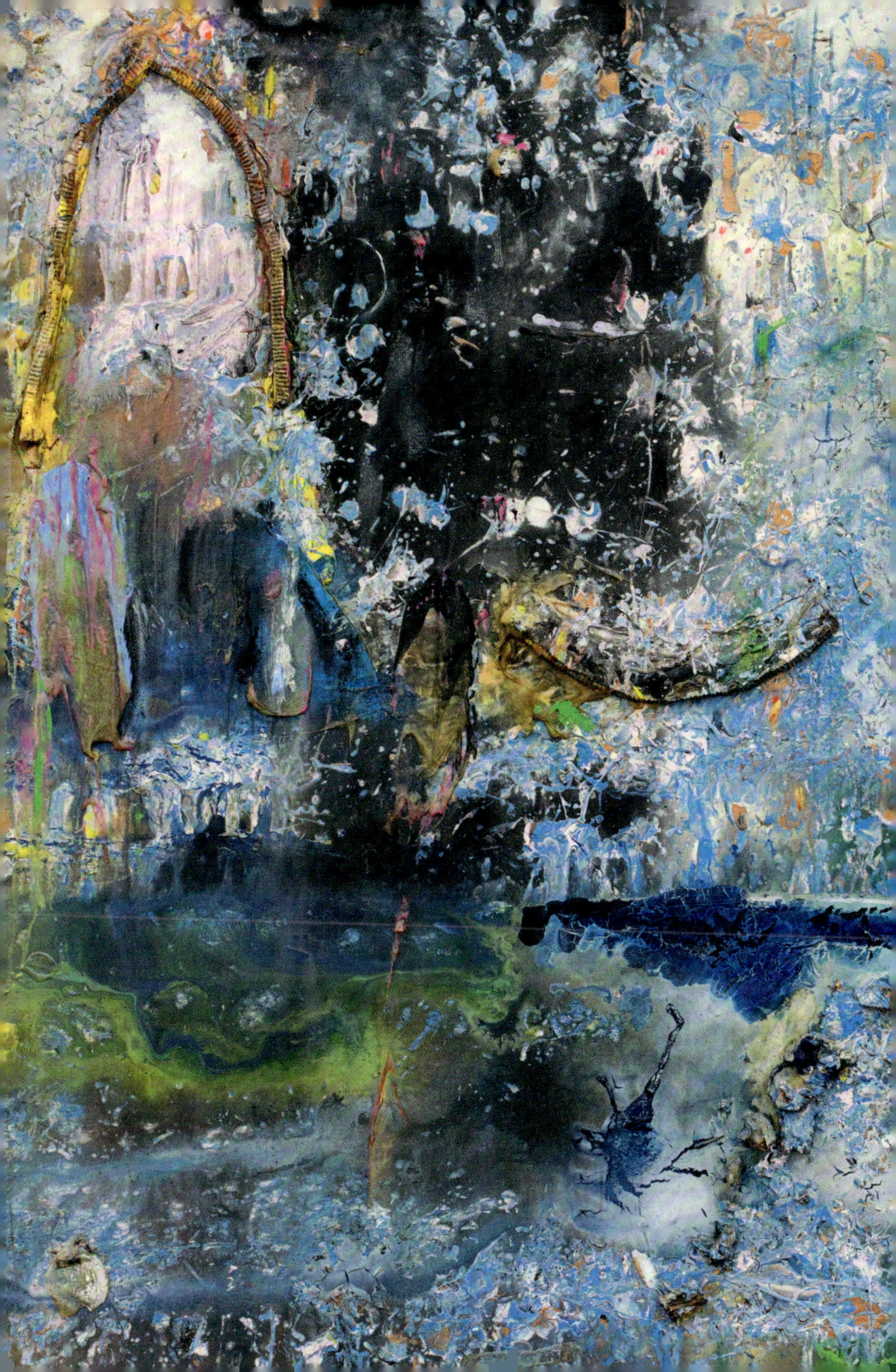

Great Thames II (detail) 1989
Acrylic paint, acrylic gel,
acrylic foam and other
materials on canvas
181 × 323.5

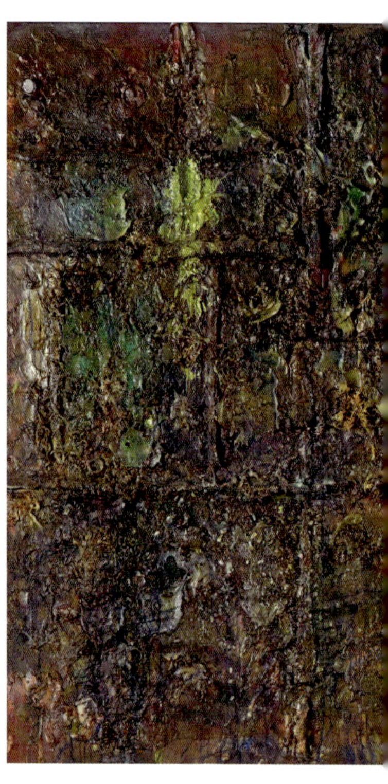

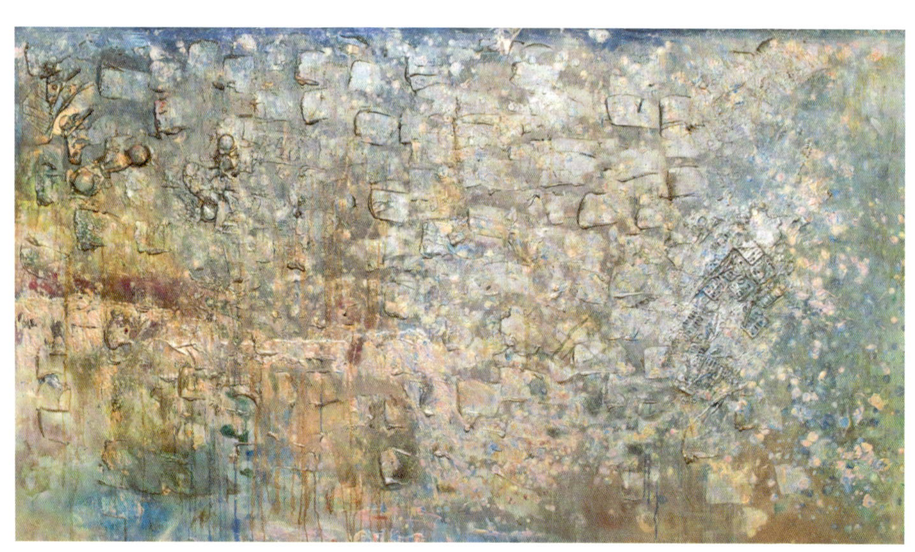

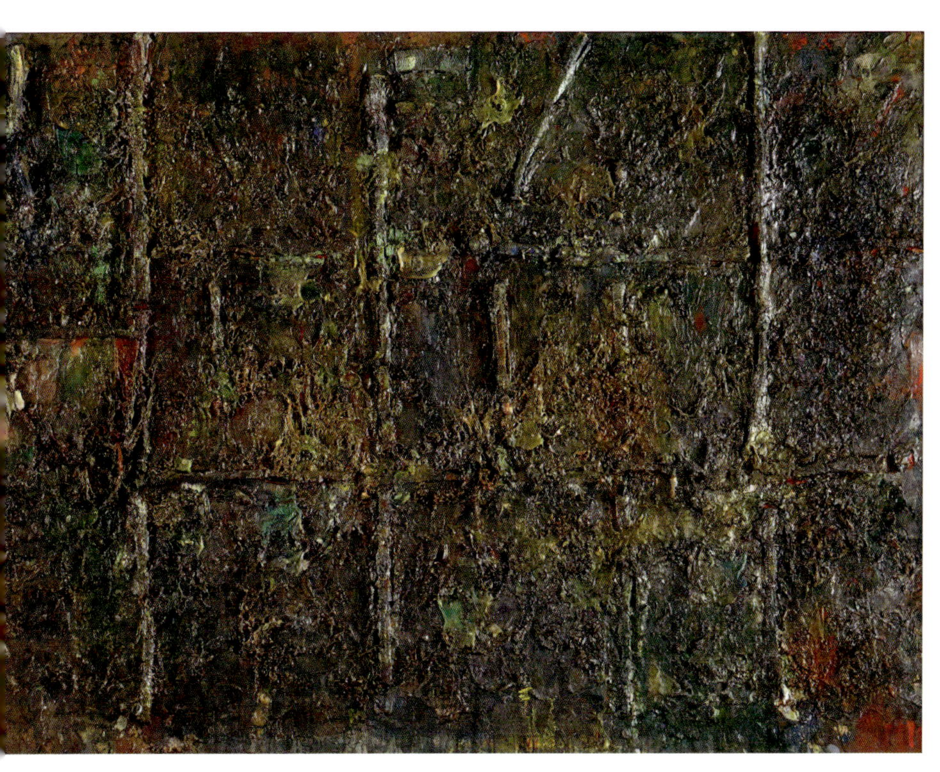

Wintergreens (detail) 1986
Acrylic paint, acrylic gel,
acrylic foam and other
materials on canvas
173 × 348

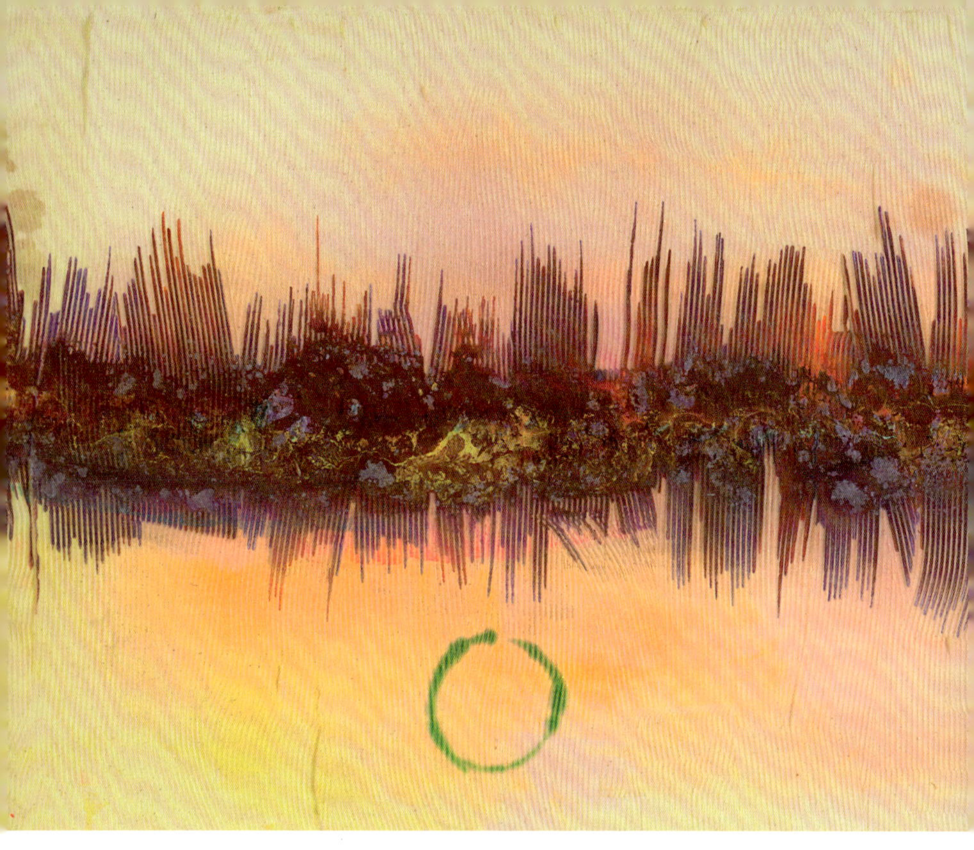

Kitty 2009
Acrylic paint on canvas
68.5 × 173

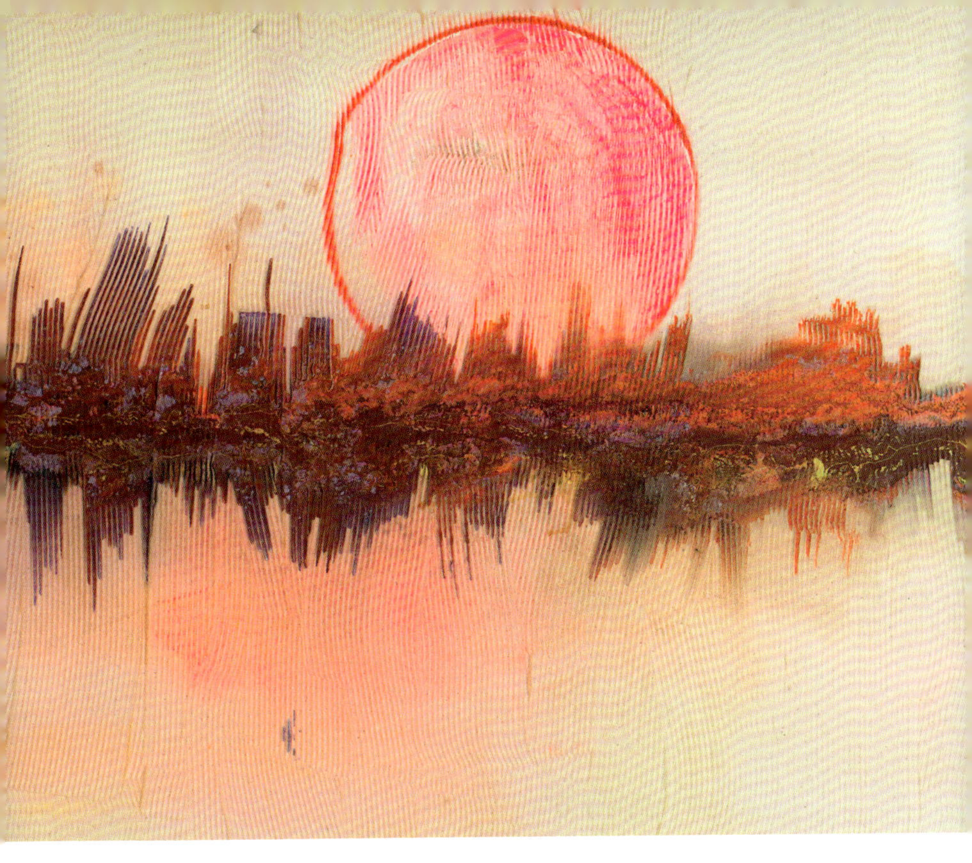

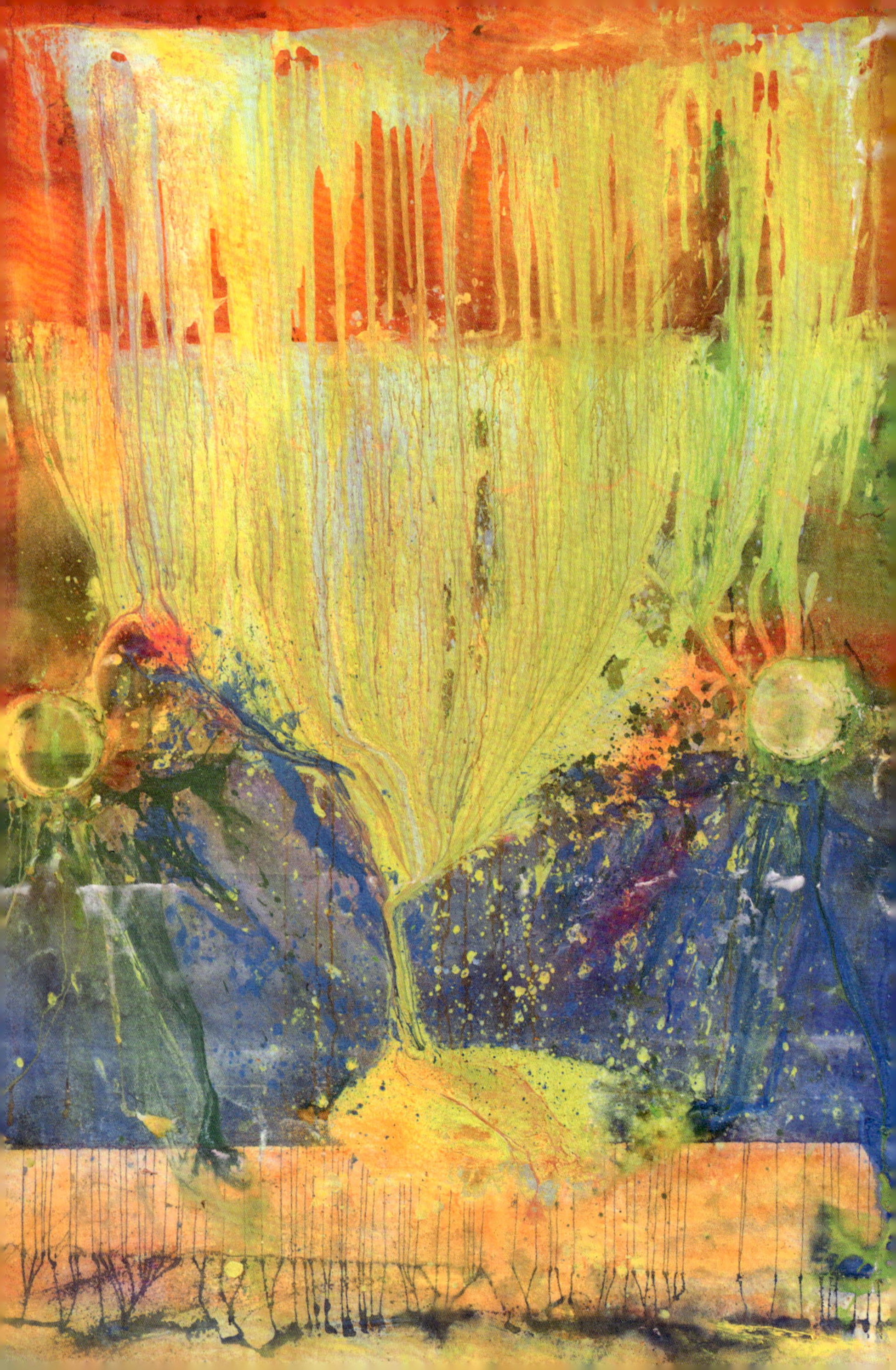

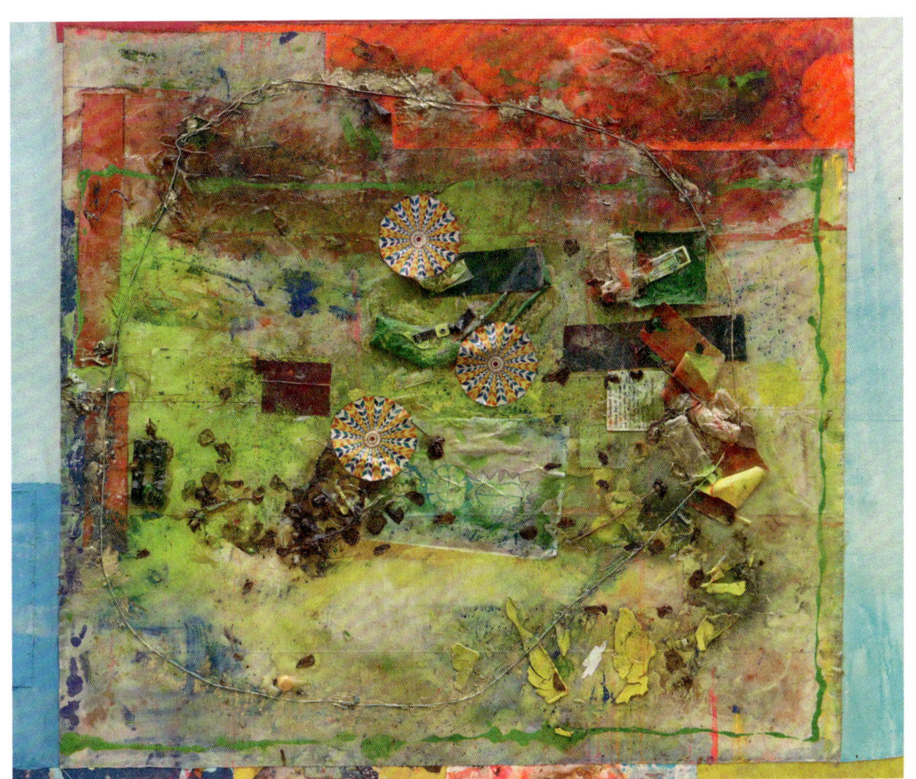

Remember Thine Eyes 2014
Acrylic paint on canvas
237.5 × 189

Mummybelli (detail) 2019
Acrylic paint, acrylic gel
and found objects on
canvas with marouflage
171.3 × 206.8

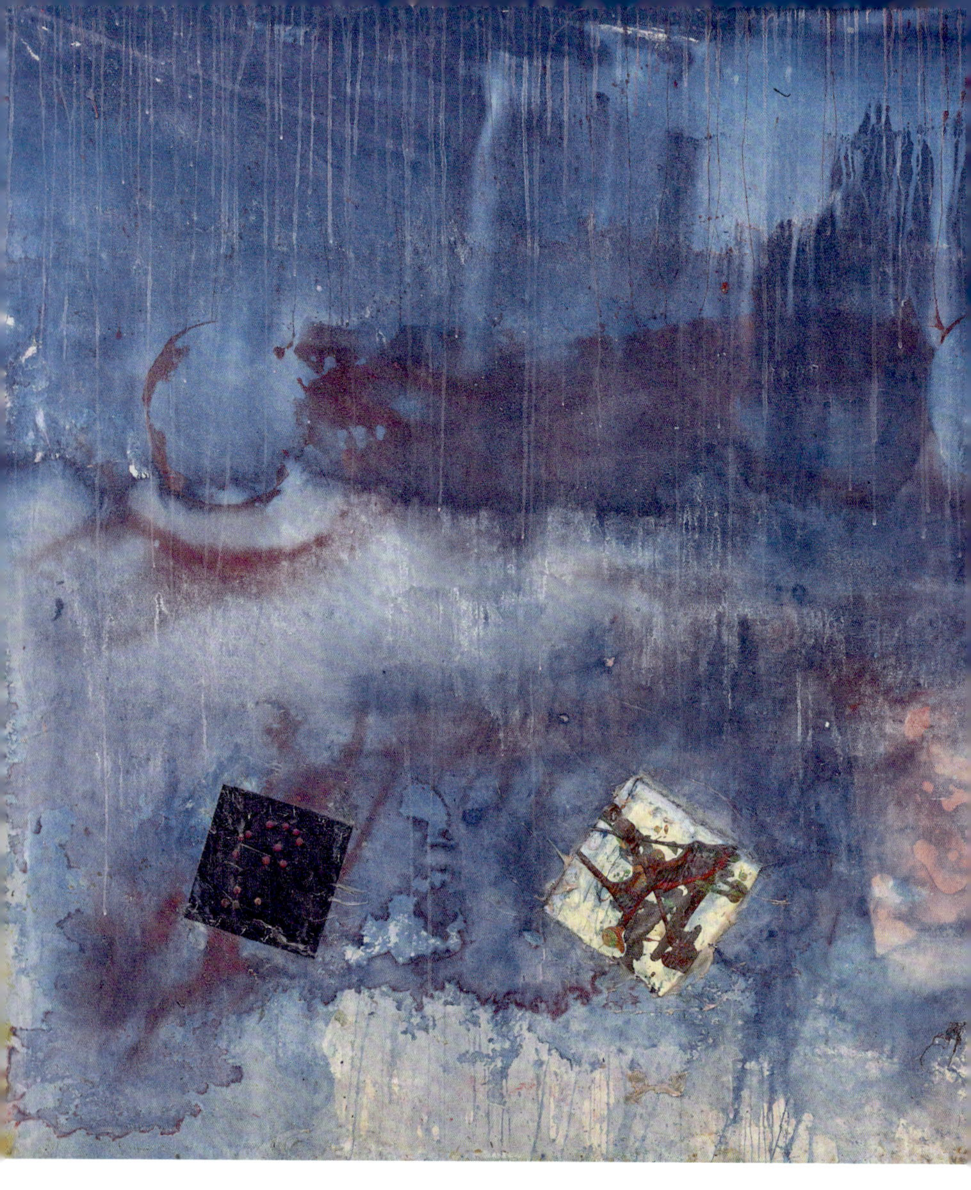

Kite One 2021
Acrylic paint, acrylic
gel and found objects
on collaged canvas with
marouflage
185.8 × 334

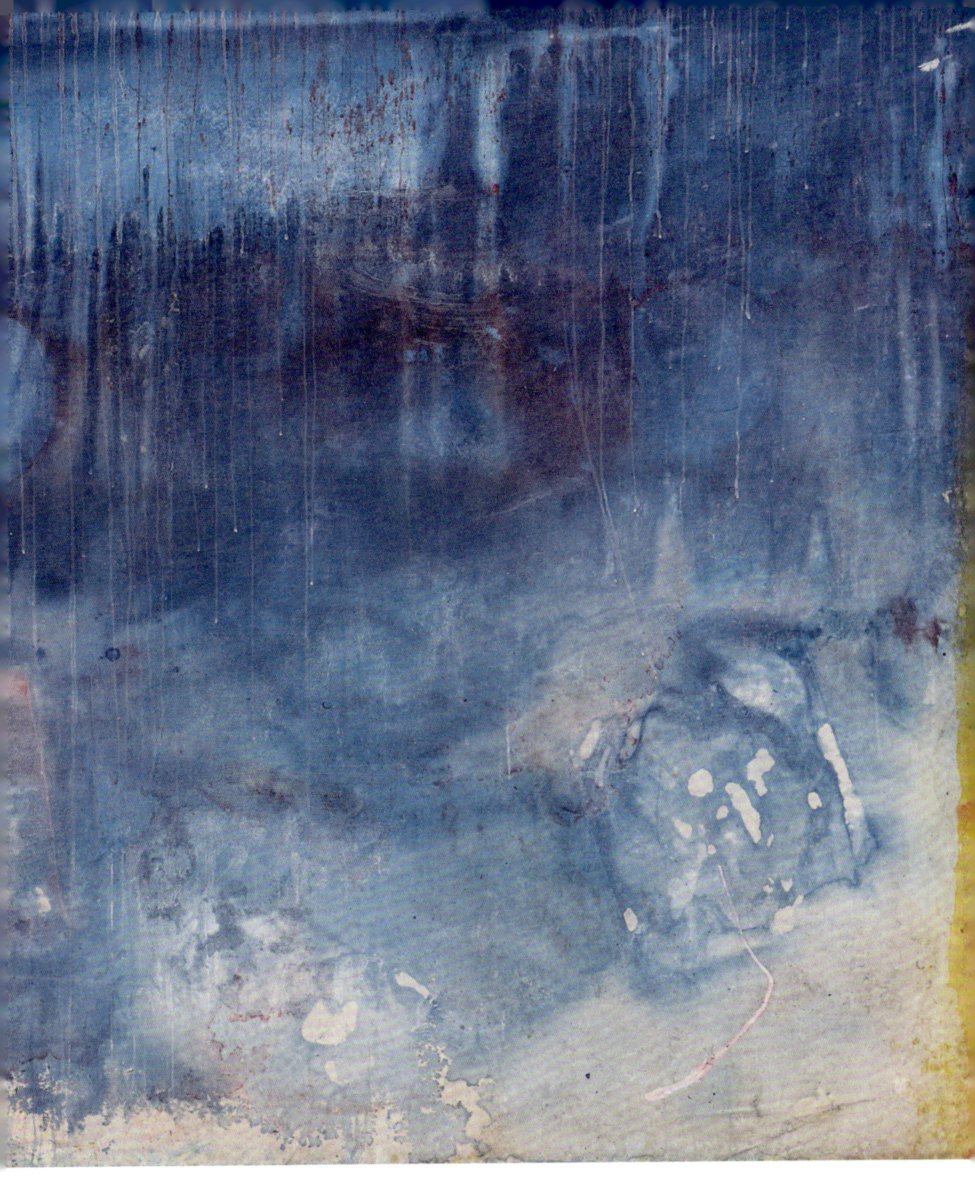

OVERLEAF
Photograph of Frank
Bowling working on
At the Window 2020 at his
studio at Peacock Yard,
London, 2020

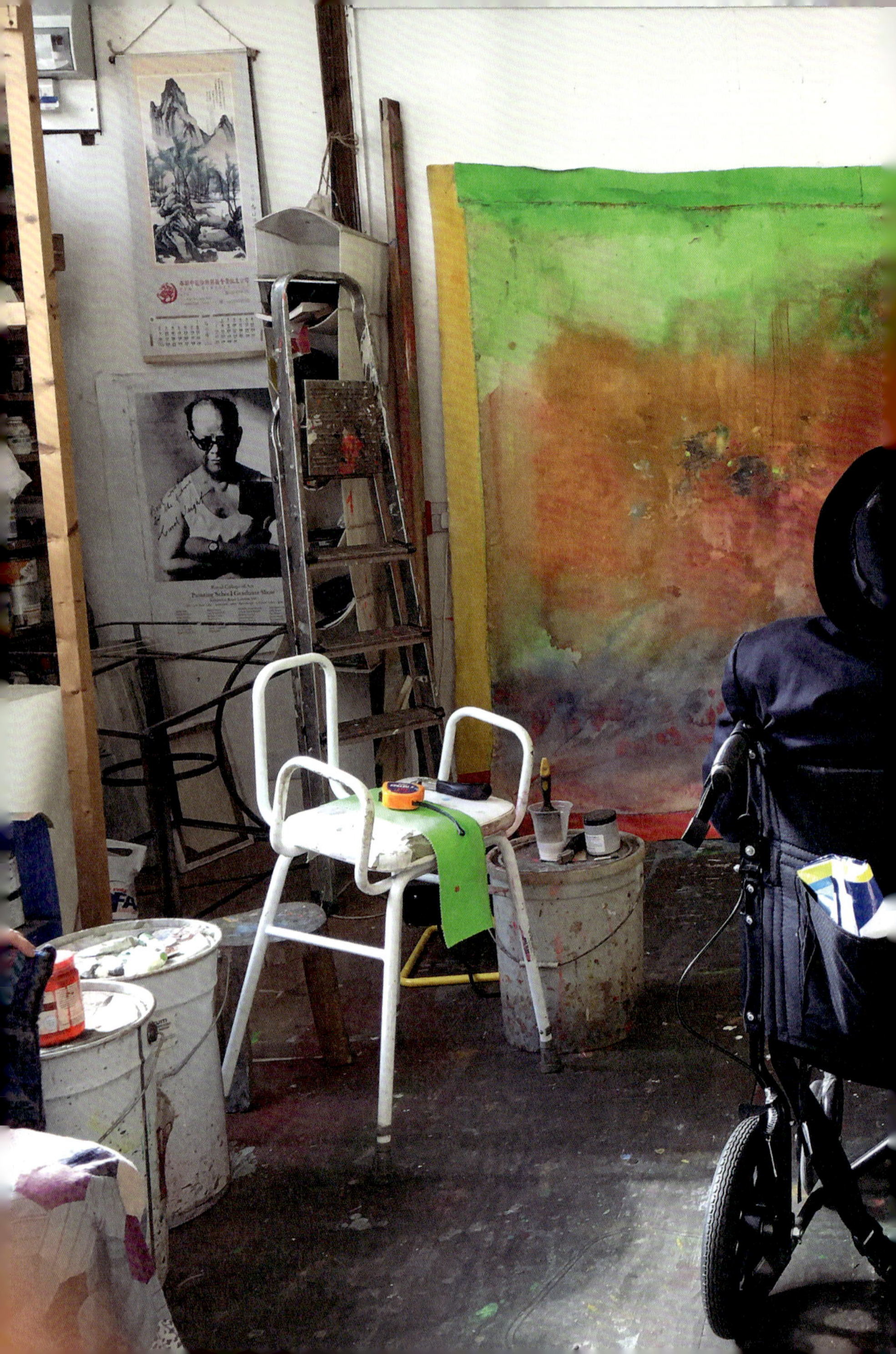

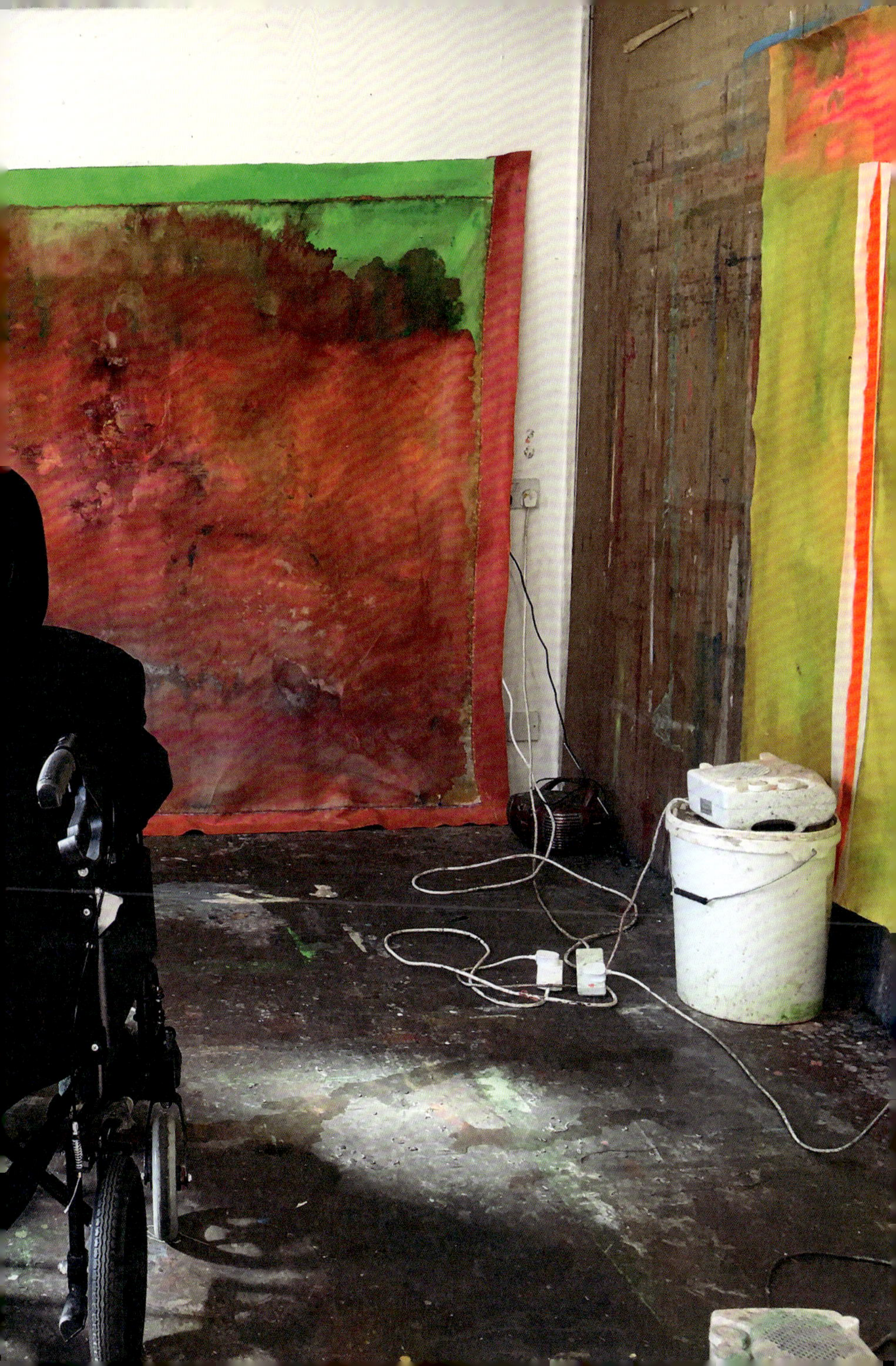

NOTES

1. Mel Gooding, *Frank Bowling*, RA Publishing, 2015, p.III.

2. Rachel Scott met Frank Bowling at the Royal College of Art as students. They reunited in 1977, becoming life partners, and married in 2013. Rachel is a textile artist and Frank's closest collaborator.

3. Kobena Mercer, 'Atlantic Errantry' in *Frank Bowling's Americas*, ed. Jennifer Snodgrass, exh. cat., Museum of Fine Arts, Boston 2022, pp.25–35.

4. Paul Gilroy, *The Black Atlantic: Modernity and Double Consciousness*, London 1993.

5. Frank Bowling to Mel Gooding, a long-standing friend and art writer, in Gooding, *Frank Bowling*, London 2021, p.14.

6. Frank Bowling, quoted in Corrine L. Jennings (ed.), *A/Cross Currents: Synthesis in African American Abstract Painting*, exh. cat., Dakar International Biennale (US participation) 1992, accessible in the Frank Bowling Archive.

7. Frank Bowling, in conversation with the author, 16 April 2025.

8. The uprising was led by Kofi Badu, a man enslaved in what is now Ghana, and forced to work in the Americas.

9. Dorothy Price, *Frank Bowling: Landscape*, exh. cat., Hauser & Wirth, Los Angeles 2023, p.11.

10. Gooding 2015, p.16; Frank Bowling, in one of several recorded conversations with Mel Gooding: 'Frank Bowling', *National Life Stories, Artists' Lives*, British Library, 2001–7.

11. Gooding 2015, p.18. Okwui Enwezor also considers the impact of Bowling's early life, cultural and historical context on his art with particular depth in 'Mappa Mundi: Frank Bowling's Cognitive Abstraction', in Enwezor (ed.), *Frank Bowling: Mappa Mundi*, exh. cat., Haus der Kunst, Munich 2017, p.16.

12. Enwezor (ed.) 2017, p.17; Gooding, 2001–7.

13. https:/thecommonwealth.org/history, accessed 4 April 2025.

14. Enwezor (ed.) 2017, p.251.

15. Gilroy 1993.

16. The iconic building was remodelled as the Design Museum in 2016.

17. Gooding, digitised file Part 3, 2001–7.

18. Enwezor (ed.) 2017, p.255.

19. Bowling participated in key projects in Africa and the Caribbean, including the first CARIFESTA Caribbean arts festival in 1972.

20. Frank Bowling, '10 Notes From a Work in Progress', 5+1 pamphlet, New York 1969.

21. All articles are reproduced in Frank Bowling, 'Selected Writings: 1969–1993', in Enwezor (ed.) 2017, pp.198–201.

22. Frank Bowling, 'Is Black Art About Color?' in *Black Life and Culture in the United States*, ed. Rhoda Lois Goldstein, New York 1971, p.320.

23. Price 2023, p.12.

24. Goldstein (ed.) 1971, p.320.

25. Facsimiles of correspondence between Bowling and Greenberg are generously included in Enwezor (ed.) 2017, pp.220–47.

26. Gooding 2021, p.104.

27. Sonia Boyce, 'From Substrate to Riverbed' in *Frank Bowling*, ed. Elena Crippa, exh. cat., Tate, London 2019, p.73. Boyce led the hugely important AHRC Black Artists and Modernism research project from 2016 to 2019.

28. The remainder of Rachel Scott's letter to Tate (see note 1) describes precise steps once colour has been flooded onto the canvas, including the application of acrylic gel; transfer of the canvas to the floor; application of carefully mixed paint, acrylic gel, ammonia and water; embedding of shells or plastic toys; and partial drying time, depending on room temperature and weather conditions. The description concludes: 'The canvas is pulled up and tacked to the wall in stages (low, middle, high). This allows the material on the canvas to move, drip, cascade and slither in a downward motion. More gel, paint, fluorescent chalk, metallic dust is applied as the work goes from stage to stage. When completely dry, oil paint is sometimes but not always applied. After the work is stretched a thinned mixture of damar crystals and distilled turps is applied. This mixture sometimes includes beeswax.'

29. Frank Bowling, in conversation with art writer Matthew Collings, in the pamphlet for the *Frank Bowling RA* exhibition at ROLLO Contemporary Art and ArtSway, London and Hampshire 2006, accessible in the Frank Bowling Archive.

30. Sam Cornish, 'Geometry' in *Frank Bowling: Sculpture*, ed. Cornish, London 2022, pp.25–33, including Bowling quotation from an interview with Louisa Buck, 'Frank Bowling: "My Art Isn't About Politics, It's About Paint"', *The Art Newspaper*, 10 June 2021.

31. Conference attendees included Lubaina Himid, Keith Piper, Claudette Johnson, and multiple other figures who are now receiving recognition for their work.

32. Enwezor (ed.) 2017, p.266.

33. Ibid., p.269.

34. These white paintings were brought together with some earlier works in the exhibition written about by Collings, 2006 (see note 29).

35. 'Allie Biswas and Thomas J. Price in Conversation', in Cornish (ed.) 2022, p.179.

36. All quotations in this section are Frank Bowling, in conversation with the author, 16 April 2025.

37. Ben Gooding is the nephew of Frank Bowling's close friend Mel Gooding, their conversations closely informing this book and many before it.

38. In 1595 Sir Walter Raleigh sought the legendary city of gold, El Dorado, and wrote *The Discovery of Guiana*, fuelling European interest in colonising the Americas.

CREDITS

All works unless specified
© Frank Bowling

INDEX

Page references in *italics* indicate images.

First published 2025 by order of the Tate Trustees
by Tate Publishing, a division of Tate Enterprises Ltd
Millbank, London SW1P 4RG
www.tate.org.uk

A catalogue record for this book is available from
the British Library

ISBN 978 1 84976 972 3

Distributed in the United States and Canada by
ABRAMS, New York

Library of Congress Control Number applied for

Commissioning Editor: Emma Poulter
Project Editor: Aki Gurung
Production: Juliette Dupire
Picture Research: Sarah Tucker
Designed by Astrid Stavro Studio
Colour reproduction by DL Imaging, London
Printed and bound in Italy by Printer Trento, S.r.l

Cover: *Middle Passage* 1970 (detail, see p.46)
Frontispiece: Photograph of Frank Bowling
working on *Arachnaphilia* 2021 with *Biter* 2021 in
the background at his studio at Peacock Yard,
London, 2020

Measurements of artworks are given in centimetres,
height before width and depth

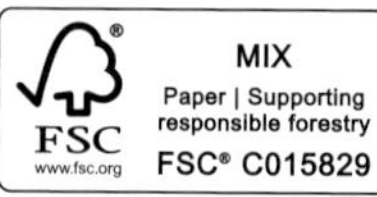

THE AUTHOR
Dominique Heyse-Moore is Senior Curator,
Contemporary British Art at Tate Britain.